A History of
Spanish Piano Music

SEIS SONATAS
PARA
CLAVE, Y FUERTE PIANO.
COMPUESTAS
POR D. MANUEL BLASCO D NEBRA
Organista de la S. Yglesia. Cathedral de Sevilla.
OBRA PRIMERA.

En Madrid

From the cover of Manuel Blasco de Nebra, *Six Sonatas for Harpsichord and Piano*, Op. 1, 1780.

A History of Spanish Piano Music

Linton E. Powell

INDIANA UNIVERSITY PRESS

BLOOMINGTON

To KATHY
For Her Constant Encouragement

Portions of chapter 4 originally appeared in the *Piano Quarterly* 101
(Winter 1975–76).

Library of Congress Cataloging in Publication Data
Powell, Linton.
A history of Spanish piano music.
Bibliography: p.
Includes index.
1. Piano music—History and criticism. 2. Music,
Spanish—History and criticism. I. Title.
ML738.P7   786.4'041'0946   79-3761
ISBN 0–253–18114–3   1 2 3 4 5   84 83 82 81 80

Contents

Preface

To my knowledge, this book is the first comprehensive survey of solo piano music in Spain from the eighteenth century to the present. Throughout this study I have tried to be as detailed as possible; however, for some very early composers as well as for some recent ones, little information is available. Four chapters emphasize the major centers of activity, composers, and their compositions for piano. A separate chapter showing the influence of the guitar on Spanish keyboard music has been added because of the significance of the guitar and its particular techniques to the general history of Spanish music. The glossary defines the numerous Spanish dances and other terminology unfamiliar to the general reader.

The appendixes will supply the reader with much-needed information regarding anthologies and modern editions of early Spanish piano music and a selective list of more recent works. Because of the wide scope of this study, it has not been possible to give exhaustive information for the later music. For that reason, I would like to list here the major publishers of Spanish piano music: Union Musical Española, Madrid; Editions Salabert, Paris; Max Eschig, Paris; Sénart, Paris; Alphonse Leduc, Paris; Rouart Lerolle, Paris; Editorial de Música Española Contemporánea, Madrid; Editorial Alpuerto, Madrid; Southern Music Publishing Company, New York; Peer International Corporation, New York; Ediciones Armónico, Barcelona; Universal Editions, Vienna; Tonos, Darmstadt; and Moeck, Celle.

I am indebted to a number of persons for their help in the preparation and completion of this project. I am especially grateful to Jean R. Longland of the Hispanic Society of America for information on piano building in Spain; Hilda McCurdy for certain French

vii

translations; Jane Clark of London for information on Scarlatti and Spanish folk music and for first directing me to the music of Albero; Almonte Howell for information on Vicente Rodríguez; John Lee for suggestions about the text; Mary Alice Price for her assistance with numerous items borrowed through Interlibrary Loan at the University of Texas at Arlington; James E. Richards for giving me research time on my faculty load; John Dowling for certain Spanish translations; and my wife, Kathy F. Powell, for her expert editorial suggestions in the text and typing of the final manuscript. I am also grateful to the following people in Spain: Maria Angela Otero of Union Musical Española, Madrid; Josefina Sastre of the library of the Orfeó Català, Barcelona; and Josefa Martorell of the Biblioteca de Catalunya, Barcelona.

I would also like to thank the American Philosophical Society and the Organized Research Fund of the University of Texas at Arlington for research grants in support of this project.

The following abbreviations are used in the text:

ed(s).	editor(s)
Ex(x).	example(s)
MS	manuscript
m(m).	measure(s)
Suppl.	supplement

Lower-case Roman numerals indicate the specific movement of a work, e.g., Sonata in C major/ii. Arabic numerals given after a slash, such as in Sonata in D major/86–90, indicate measure numbers.

A system of short-title references has been used in the text and notes. Complete information on each reference can be found in the Bibliography.

A HISTORY OF
SPANISH PIANO MUSIC

CHAPTER ONE

Early Spanish Piano Music, 1740–1840

Introduction

The history of Spanish piano music is not one of a solid, steadily progressive tradition. Spain produced great composers of sacred vocal polyphony, vihuela music, and organ music in the sixteenth century, its golden age of composition. Notable among the organ composers was Antonio de Cabezón. The seventeenth century featured such Spanish organists/composers as José Jiménez, Pablo Bruna, and Juan Cabanilles. Even in the eighteenth century, the era when the piano was invented and gradually took on prominence all over Europe, Spain continued with its tradition of organ music, over three hundred works having been written by the noted José Elías. While the piano was in use in certain areas of Spain as early as the 1740s, the organ was more readily available to the numerous organists/priests, who made up the majority of the native Spanish composers for keyboard of the period.

Besides the organ, the harpsichord (*clave, clavicordio,* or *clavicímbalo*) and piano (*fuerte piano* or *piano forte*) are specified in the titles of Spanish keyboard music in the eighteenth century; e.g., Sebastián de Albero's *Obras para clavicordio o piano forte* and Blasco de Nebra's *Seis sonatas para clave y fuerte piano.*[1]

Many works, of course, do not name an instrument, but may have a title such as *Sonata de clarines* (by Soler), which indicates trumpet stops on the Spanish organ. However, the composition may clearly be in a lighter style more closely associated with the harpsichord or piano and not at all akin to imitative organ works such as the *tiento*. Thus, numerous works entitled "sonata" or "rondo" written by a host of Spanish organists/priests may indeed be organ works, but they strongly suggest a style more suited to stringed keyboard instruments and were probably performed on such instruments when available. One must realize this flexibility when approaching Spanish keyboard music of the eighteenth and early nineteenth centuries.

Other factors also affected the course of Spanish piano music during the first hundred years of its evolution. In the late eighteenth century, the *zarzuela* became more "popular" in nature, but eventually it was eclipsed by the ever-increasing preponderance of Italian opera and the rise of the *tonadilla escénica*. Italian opera began to take a stranglehold in Spain as far back as the singer Farinelli. Gilbert Chase states that shortly after the arrival of Farinelli in Madrid (1737), the royal theater of the Buen Retiro became a veritable fortress of Italianism.[2]

The early nineteenth century was a time of great change for Spain. She was dragged into disastrous wars; she was invaded by Napoleon, who installed his own brother as the new monarch; and she suffered at the hands of her own Fernando VII. Revolution and anarchy kept her in constant upheaval. During this period, Spanish lyric theater continued to decline. By the 1830s, Spain's native lyric theater was virtually nonexistent. The *zarzuela* had disappeared and the *tonadilla* had run its course. However, the popularity of Italian opera continued to rise in Spain.

During this "tug-of-war" between native Spanish music and Italian music, what of Spanish harpsichord and piano music? While Bach, Haydn, Mozart, Beethoven, and Chopin were writing their masterworks for harpsichord or piano, who were the major Spanish keyboard composers?

Apparently no harpsichord music was printed in Spain in the first part of the eighteenth century, the earliest of the century being Juan Sessé's *Seis fugas para órgano y clave* of 1773. However, there are some small works for harpsichord preserved in a manuscript collection in the Biblioteca Nacional of Madrid entitled *Libro de música de clavicímbalo del S^r. D^n. Francisco de Tejada 1721.* Most of the 83 compositions in this collection are anonymous and quite simple in construction. Of the 45 minuets, many have titles such as *Dueña hermosa* ("Beautiful Mistress") or *Triste memoria* ("Sad Memory").[3] These works pose a timid contrast to the magnificent works we are about to encounter by one of the most remarkable keyboard composers of all times, Domenico Scarlatti.

Madrid, Valencia, Málaga, and the Escorial

Any history of Spanish piano music must by necessity begin with DOMENICO SCARLATTI (1685–1757), the noted Italian cembalist who lived most of his productive life as a musician in Spain. Few Spanish keyboard composers after him have escaped his influence.

Domenico Scarlatti was born of a Sicilian family in Naples. He visited Florence in 1702, stayed in Venice for four years from 1705 to 1709, served in Rome for ten years until 1719, and then probably went directly to Lisbon. While in Lisbon, one of his main duties was to teach the daughter, Maria Barbara, as well as the younger brother of King John V of Portugal. Upon the marriage of Maria Barbara to Fernando, heir to the throne of Spain, in 1729, Scarlatti followed in her service to Seville, and from there to Madrid in 1733, where he remained until his death.

Scarlatti composed more than a dozen operas and several church compositions before he left Italy. However, none of his keyboard compositions can be placed with certainty before he reached the age of 40 and his service in Portugal. Except for a few fugues and dances, his important output in keyboard music consists of sonatas.[4] Scarlatti composed some 550 sonatas, according to the noted scholar Ralph Kirkpatrick.[5] The earliest sonatas, 30 in number, were published in London in late 1738 or early 1739 with the title *Essercizi per gravicembalo*. This edition was followed in 1739 by Roseingrave's publication of 32 more sonatas under the title *Suite de pièces pour le clavecin*.[6] However, the majority of the sonatas remained in manuscript during Scarlatti's lifetime. They are preserved in four huge collections, with much overlapping of contents, in Venice, Parma, Münster, and Vienna.

Although Scarlatti employed the title *Essercizi* ("Exercises") for his publication of 1738, the individual pieces he labeled *sonatas*. Occasionally he would use other designations, such as *toccata, fugue, pastorale, aria, capriccio, minuet, gavotte,* or *gigue*; but generally throughout his total output, the term *sonata* was used.

For Scarlatti, *sonata* seems to indicate a one-movement composition in binary form, though a few early works are in several movements. However, some scholars contend that many of his sonatas were grouped in pairs or even in threes and were intended to be performed as such.

Ralph Kirkpatrick states,

> The Scarlatti sonata is a piece in binary form, divided into two halves by a double bar, of which the first half announces a basic tonality and then moves to establish the closing tonality of the double bar (dominant, relative major or minor, in a few cases the relative minor of the dominant) in a series of decisive cadences; and of which the second half departs from the tonic of the double bar, eventually to reestablish the basic tonic in a series of equally decisive cadences, making use of the same thematic material that was used for the establishment of the closing tonality at the end of the first half. . . . The only thematic material that is nearly always subject to more or less exact restatement is that which is associated with those sections at the end of each half which establish the closing tonality.[7]

For this parallelism of cadential material, Kirkpatrick has coined the term *crux*. According to his definition, there is a point in each half of a sonata where the thematic material that is stated in parallel fashion at the ends of both halves establishes the closing tonality of each half.[8] Thus, the crux is always dependent on these two factors—establishment of the closing tonality and establishment of thematic parallelism between the two halves.[9] For illustrations of the crux, see Exx. 1 and 2.

Ex. 1. Scarlatti, Sonata in A minor (K. 3/L. 378).

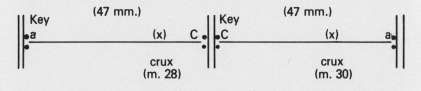

Ex. 2. Scarlatti, Sonata in A minor (K. 3/L. 378). Used by permission of Belwin Mills Publishing Corp.

Although we know that the new, expressive pianoforte was available in Spain to Scarlatti, we have reason to believe that he preferred the harpsichord.[10] Queen Maria Barbara, Scarlatti's employer, owned twelve keyboard instruments, five of which were pianofortes made in Florence, probably by Cristofori or his pupil Ferrini. Each of the palaces at Aranjuez and Escorial had a pianoforte. However, there is little evidence that Scarlatti was in any way tempted to abandon the harpsichord for the pianoforte. Most of his later sonatas extended beyond the range of the queen's pianofortes. Moreover, the early piano lacked the power and brilliance of the harpsichords known to Scarlatti. Kirkpatrick is of the opinion that the pianoforte was used at the Spanish court largely for accompanying, since Farinelli was fond of it, and that the harpsichord retained its superiority for solo music.[11]

Scarlatti treated the harpsichord in a highly idiomatic manner, which often requires great skill on the part of the performer. Patterns of brilliant figurations, arpeggios, wide leaps, rapid repeated notes, and hand-crossings all contribute to this unmistakable keyboard style.[12] The difficult type of hand-crossing can be seen in Ex. 3.

Ex. 3.   Scarlatti, Sonata in D minor (K. 120/L. 215)/36–41. © 1953 G. Schirmer, Inc. Used by permission.

Scarlatti also uses the harpsichord to emulate various timbres. A glissando appears in the Sonata in F major (K. 379/L. 73)—an ascending scale is marked *con dedo solo* ("with one finger"). Fanfare trumpet or horn themes abound in the sonatas, e.g., K. 96/L. 465, K. 119/L. 415; and the illusion of flutes and bagpipes (K. 513/L. suppl. 3) or bells (K. 482/L. 205) can also be found. Scarlatti often wished to suggest the strumming of the guitar, either by rapid repeated chords, often with dissonant percussive *acciaccature,* or by a swiftly repeated figuration in the bass.[13]

That Scarlatti was influenced by Spanish folk music is very evident in his sonatas. Dr. Charles Burney, on one of his famous musical tours in Europe, met a certain Monsieur l'Augier, who had been a close acquaintance of Scarlatti. Burney reports, "There are many pages in Scarlatti's pieces in which he imitates the melody of tunes sung by carriers, muleteers, and common people."[14] We must not forget that Maria Barbara, Scarlatti's employer, spent the first four years of her new life in Spain in Seville, and that during that time the court moved about various cities of Andalusia. Apparently, the very striking folk music of this region made an indelible impression on Scarlatti.[15]

Andalusian folk music is known the world over for its characteristic Phrygian sound, using the descending tetrachord la–sol–fa–mi or A–G–F–E; and for its Morrish version A–G-sharp–F–E. Scarlatti employed these scalar traits in many of his sonatas, but the Andalusian characteristics go beyond these patterns. The *saeta* is a form of *cante* improvised in the streets of Seville during the Holy Week processions. It is accompanied by a drum beating the rhythmic pattern ♩ ♪♩♪ ♩ . Scarlatti's Sonata in D major, K. 490/L. 206, is clearly a *saeta.* (See Ex. 4.)

Many other sonatas by Scarlatti reflect the ravishing, exotic sounds associated with folk music of Andalusia. Sonata K. 492/L. 14 has the characteristics of a *bulerías;* Sonata K. 502/L. 3 a *peteneras;* and Sonata K. 105/L. 204 the *jota,* to name only a few.

VICENTE RODRÍGUEZ (c.1685–1760), probably the first *native* Spaniard to write keyboard sonatas, spent nearly 48 years as

Ex. 4. Scarlatti, Sonata in D major (K. 490/L. 206)/71–80. © 1953 G. Schirmer, Inc. Used by permission.

priest and organist at Valencia Cathedral. He was appointed to the post in 1713 upon the death of Juan Cabanilles, and held it until his own death on December 15, 1760.

It is not known whether Rodríguez already knew some of Scarlatti's sonatas, such as the published *Essercizi* of 1738. William S. Newman contends that "it is more likely that this cleric, at his restricted post, was giving good evidence of how far such forms and styles had developed in the peninsula independently of Scarlatti's arrival."[16]

For many years the only work known by V. Rodríguez was the Sonata in F major published by Joaquin Nin in Vol. II of his *Classiques espagnols du piano*, 1929.[17] However, it has now come to light that a harpsichord manuscript of 31 sonatas resides at the library of the Orfeó Català in Barcelona.[18]

The title page of the Rodríguez collection reads as follows:

LIBRO
DE TOCATAS PARA CIMBALO
REPARTIDAS
POR TODOS LOS PUNTOS DE UN DIAPASON,
Con la advertencia, que por todas las teclas blancas estan por
tersera menor, y tercera mayor á excepcion de las ne-

gras, que por lo desasinado de los Terminos, no
estan mas, que por el que menos disuena.
COMPUESTO
POR M. VISENTE RODRIGUEZ PRESBITERO
Organista Principal de la Metropolitana Yglesia de Valencia.
Año 1744.[19]

The opening of the title, *Libro de Tocatas,* might seem confusing at first, but not if we remember that the words *toccata* and *sonata* were regularly interchangeable in this period, and not if we note that each piece is designated *sonata* within the manuscript.

The collection contains thirty sonatas followed by a two-movement *Pastorela* in G major, which is in effect a thirty-first sonata. The total number of pieces is forty-four, with the majority being one-movement sonatas. Ten are multi-movement; of these, seven have two movements in the order slow–fast, and three have three movements in the order fast–slow–fast. In a few cases, movements lead directly from one to another and are incomplete by themselves.

Sixteen of the individual movements are in the Scarlatti bipartite form, all but one of these constituting single-movement sonatas. As with Scarlatti, the first half cadences on the dominant or relative major, and the halves are generally balanced, though at times the second half is greatly expanded through development. Ex. 5 is taken from the opening of the stately Sonata in A-flat major, one of V. Rodríguez's most attractive works.[20]

A number of the remaining works have been categorized by Almonte Howell according to familiar compositional types: (1) concerto–ritornello: recurring theme of tutti character separated by solo-like figural episodes; (2) etude or toccata: *perpetuum mobile* figure that gives rise to varied forms of related figures in continuous motor activity; (3) invention: theme and countertheme alternate between the hands. A few movements begin with quasi-fugal expositions, though, as in Scarlatti, fugal procedures are never maintained for long.

Howell states that V. Rodríguez, like many transitional figures,

Ex. 5.   V. Rodríguez, Sonata in A-flat major/1–11. Copyright © 1975
Willy Mueller, Sueddeutscher Musikverlag, Heidelberg. Used by permission of C.F. Peters Corporation, New York.

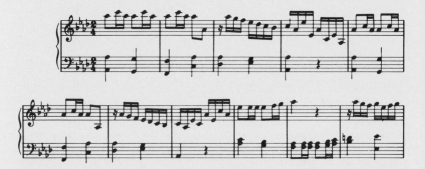

tries to enjoy the best of both worlds—Baroque and Classic. But
within this fluctuation, he is not totally successful. He tends to
carry on figurations and sequences much too long and to wander
harmonically with no clear sense of tonal goal. Anyone who has
examined Spanish keyboard music of the seventeenth and early
eighteenth centuries will find these "faults"—long-windedness and
harmonic meandering. They appear to be native Spanish traits,
endemic to the music. But, as Howell states, perhaps they are deliberate esthetic aims. Could centuries of intimate exposure to an
alien Near Eastern culture have left a lingering fondness among the
Spanish people for the static, the contemplative, the immobile, the
goal-less, in contrast to Westerners' continual haste to be in motion
from one preplanned point to another through the most efficient
means of transport? At any rate, we have not seen the last of this
characteristic in Spanish keyboard music.

   Padre RAFAEL ANGLÉS (c.1730–1816) was a native of Rafales
in the province of Teruel; he eventually became Chapelmaster of
the Alcañiz (Teruel) Collegiate. In April 1761 he competed with
other musicians for the organist position recently vacated by V.
Rodríguez in Valencia. The chair was won by Manuel Narro, a Valencian whose technique was supposedly equal to that of Anglés.
According to the committee of judges, Anglés was ahead of his

time—"he exceeds in modern style." Apparently, to them, this "modern style" was not in keeping with the traditional music of the church.[21] Nevertheless, on February 8 of the following year, Anglés was named first organist of Valencia Cathedral, where he remained until his death.[22]

Nin, in Vol. II of *Classiques espagnols du piano,* made available the following works by Anglés: Adagietto in B-flat major, Sonata in F major, Aria in D minor, and Fugatto in B-flat major.[23] In 1970, Sonata in E minor and another Sonata in F major were published by Union Musical Española, José Climent, editor.

All three sonatas by Anglés are in binary form. The one in F major (from the Nin collection) and the one in E minor (Climent edition) are of the Scarlattian crux type, whereas Sonata in F major from the Climent edition shows the influence of the more modern sonata–allegro form, complete with exposition, development, and recapitulation. This third sonata shows other "modern" tendencies in that Anglés has placed *piano* and *forte* markings within the opening phrases of the work, probably indicating the piano rather than the harpsichord or the organ.[24] See Ex. 6.

The Adagietto in B-flat major is also in binary form and of the Scarlattian crux type. This work exhibits, as does the Sonata in F major from the Nin collection, Anglés' penchant for fluctuation of mode.

Ex. 6.   Anglés, Sonata in F major (Climent edition)/1–7. © 1970. Used by permission of the publisher, Union Musical Española.

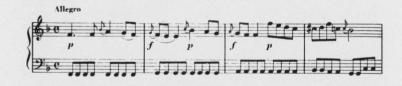

The influence of Haydn is evident in all the aforementioned works except the Aria in D minor. Here we find Anglés reaching back to Bach's Italian style to produce a singing melody over a slow-moving bass. It is one of the most beautiful pieces of its type in the Spanish literature.

SEBASTIÁN DE ALBERO (1722–1756), of Roncal, Navarra, was one of the most promising talents in Spain during the eighteenth century. Unfortunately, he died at the early age of 34. Having been named first organist of the Royal Chapel in 1746 at age 24, he was a musician in the service of Fernando VI, which places him in the circle of Scarlatti.[25]

An undated manuscript at the Biblioteca del Real Conservatorio Superior de Música in Madrid contains some of Albero's keyboard works. It is entitled *Obras para clavicordio o piano forte* and is dedicated to Fernando VI. Since Albero died in 1756 and Fernando VI was king from 1746 to 1759, the works must have been written between 1746 and 1756. A likely date would be 1746, the year Albero was appointed first organist to the Royal Chapel. The collection might have been a special gift to the king in appreciation for his employment. In any event, these works seem to be the earliest in Spain that specifically indicate "piano" in the title.

The first use of the words *piano e forte* in a title was by the Italian Lodovico Giustini of Pistoia in 1732 in his *Sonate da cimbalo di piano e forte detto volgarmente di martelletti*.[26] However, the word *pianoforte,* or some similar usage, did not appear regularly in titles of keyboard music in Spain or elsewhere until the 1760s; in Spain, this trend was represented by some minuets by Joaquín Montero dated 1764. The earliest use of the word in France was by Nicholas Séjan in 1765, and in England by John Burton in 1766. The early use of *piano forte* in the title by Albero indicates that Spain was keeping abreast of the times, if not a bit ahead of other parts of Europe in this particular instance.

Each work by Albero in the manuscript collection in Madrid has the unusual title *Recercata, fuga y sonata.*[27] From the two works available for study in modern edition, one can see that the term *recercata* implies the improvisatory type of sixteenth-century lute *ricercar* with free sequential passages, much like a prelude. Both *recercatas* by Albero have a meter signature of **C** but no bar lines. Although specific note values are used, there is no doubt that the work was intended to be performed in a free, somewhat improvisational manner, similar to the preludes of Louis Couperin, although L. Couperin's preludes have no time signatures and all notes are written as being equal in value.

Both *recercatas* are in the minor mode and tend to linger on the raised fourth and seventh degrees of the scale, giving the works a biting, pungent quality. Harmonically, they are very adventuresome. The *Recercata* in C minor briefly touches on B minor, C-sharp minor, and A minor in its middle section; and the *Recercata* in D minor has a striking enharmonic modulation to F-sharp minor from E-flat major, as seen in Ex. 7.

Ex. 7   Albero, *Recercata* in D minor/middle section. © 1977. Used by permission of the publisher, Union Musical Española.

The fugues tend to be a bit long and tedious; e.g., the Fugue in D minor is 300 measures long, and the Fugue in C minor, 451 measures. Moreover, the Fugue in D minor has a basic eighth-note movement in 6/8 with no rhythmic variety. However, it does have a rhythmically stirring conclusion over a pedal point. In the Fugue in C minor, shorter note values begin to give some rhythmic relief a little over halfway through (m. 259). Again, there is an exciting finish, this time with an interesting use of the low register of the keyboard.

The two sonatas are of the Scarlatti binary design with crux. The harmonic boldness of the *recercatas* carries over somewhat into the sonatas, and the Sonata in D major smacks again of Scarlatti, with its folk influence and *acciaccature*. See Ex. 8.

Ex. 8.   Albero, Sonata in D major/86–90. © 1977. Used by permission of the publisher, Union Musical Española.

A separate collection of 30 sonatas (*Sonatas para Clavicordio*) by Albero can be found in Venice manuscript 9768,[28] which was apparently copied by the same scribe who copied the Parma manuscript of Scarlatti and most of his works in Venice manuscripts 9770–9784. Joel Sheveloff, who has made a thematic index of these 30 sonatas by Albero,[29] states, "the harmonic language, phrasing, form, motivic development and keyboard technique are quite close to Scarlatti, though the quality of the sonatas does not quite reach that of his master."[30] Sheveloff even goes so far as to say that Albero may very well be the nearest disciple to Scarlatti's unique style.

Though I would not regard Albero in quite that light, the influence of Scarlatti's techniques is readily apparent in both sets of sonatas by Albero. What was the real relationship between Maria Barbara's established composer of sonatas and the young organist of the Royal Chapel? Was Albero a disciple, collaborator, or rival of Scarlatti at the court of Fernando VI? We do not know the answer, but it is interesting to note that on the dedication page of the Madrid manuscript, Albero does not mention the name of the queen, Maria Barbara, who was a noted keyboard student of Scarlatti. This fact might suggest a rivalry, but perhaps Albero was intentionally devoting all his attention to the king in appreciation for his employment.[31]

Padre ANTONIO SOLER (1729–1783), one of Spain's chief keyboard composers in the eighteenth century, was born in the Catalonian town of Olot de Porrera. At the age of six, he was admitted to the famed Escolania of Montserrat, where he made rapid progress with his musical studies. In 1752, at age 23, he became a monk and was appointed organist and choirmaster at the Escorial monastery northwest of Madrid.

It was during the first five years at the Escorial that Soler supposedly received instruction from Scarlatti. On the title page of a collection of Soler's sonatas the composer is described as "discepolo de Domenico Scarlatti";[32] also, an autograph of 27 sonatas that Soler gave to Lord Fitzwilliam of Cambridge bears the following note written and signed by Lord Fitzwilliam: "The original of these harpsichord lessons was given to me by Father Soler at the Escorial, 14th February, 1772; Father Soler had been instructed by Scarlatti." From these sonatas came the posthumous and only eighteenth-century publication of Soler's sonatas. They were issued by Birchall of London, probably in 1796.

When Scarlatti died in 1757, Soler took over his duties as keyboard tutor to the royal family and as the supplier of sonatas for Scarlatti's pupils. Presumably, Soler wrote most of his keyboard works for the Infante Gabriel of Bourbon.[33]

The Scarlatti-type sonata evidently served as the model for Soler.[34] Soler employed the one-movement form cast in binary design. However, as with Scarlatti, many of the sonatas appear to fall into groups of two or more movements.[35] The internal structure of a typical Soler sonata is usually very close to that of a Scarlatti sonata, complete with crux. Ex. 9 shows Soler's use of the principle of the crux.

Ex. 9.   Soler, Sonata in D major (R. 84).

In many of the Soler sonatas, one finds the same technical devices as those employed by Scarlatti; e.g., repeated notes and hand-crossings (Ex. 10). Soler also employs such Scarlattian devices as difficult trills (R. 10), passages in thirds (R. 17), large skips and octaves (R. 10), and even a glissando (R. 66/i).

Ex. 10.   Soler, Sonata in B minor (R. 10)/29–36. © 1957. Used by permission of the publisher, Union Musical Española.

Although Soler has not proven to be an innovator in form, he does demonstrate originality in his modulations. That is not surprising when we consider that he wrote an important theoretical work, *Llave de la modulación y antigüedades de la música* (Madrid, 1762), which reveals his advanced ideas on modulation.[36] Besides writing about music, Soler invented and built musical instruments. He constructed a string and keyboard instrument that he called *afinador* (tuner) or *templante* (temperer), which was intended to make evident the division of a tone into nine parts, or commas.

Occasionally, Soler betrays a more *galant* style than did Scarlatti, as seen in his Sonatas R. 41 and R. 66. Newman finds other signs of this style and of a later generation than Scarlatti in the "comical bits of melody in the deep supporting basses (R. 10), cadential trills on penultimate dominant notes (as at the double-bars in R. 3), and the melodic appoggiaturas and feminine endings (as in R. 1 and at the double-bars in R. 56, another remarkably modern sounding, complete 'sonata form')."[37] Ex. 11 shows Soler's mid-century *galant* style.

Ex. 11. Soler, Sonata in F major (R. 56)/1–9. © 1958. Used by permission of the publisher, Union Musical Española.

Soler manifests his Spanish heritage in many of his sonatas. Native dance rhythms can be observed in Sonata in D minor, R. 24, a *soleares;* Sonata in G major, R. 4, a *bolero;* Sonata in C-sharp minor, R. 21, a *polo;* and Sonata in F-sharp major, R. 90, a *seguidilla* (Ex. 12).

Ex. 12.   Soler, Sonata in F-sharp major (R. 90)/9–17. © 1959. Used by permission of the publishers, Union Musical Española.

Soler also wrote a work for keyboard entitled *Fandango*, built on an ostinato figuration in the lower register that provides the basis for variation above it. It is one of his most colorful works, replete with guitar and castanet effects. See Ex. 13.

Ex. 13.   Soler, *Fandango*/77–86. © 1971. Used by permission of the publisher, Union Musical Española.

Although Scarlatti might not have preferred the new, expressive pianofortes because of their limited range or lack of brilliance compared to the larger harpsichords, by the 1760s and 1770s, as the piano became more popular throughout Europe, newer and larger models might have been imported to the Escorial, and Soler could have written his sonatas for the new, popular instrument of the day.

The earliest piano building in Spain seems to be that of Antonio Enríquez. In 1780, he constructed in Zaragoza some *címbalos* or *claves* in imitation of the *pianos fortes* in Holland and England. In Seville in 1783, Juan del Mármol, builder of harpsichords, made some *pianos grandes de orquesta*. Between the years 1784 and 1787 in Madrid, Francisco Flores constructed pianos in the English style. He was thought to be one of the best piano builders of the time and consequently supplied pianos for the principal homes of the court.[38]

JOAQUÍN OXINAGA (1719–1789) held various organ posts—Burgos, Bilbao, Toledo, and the Royal Chapel in Madrid. His Sonata in C major and two short minuets are now in modern edition.[39]

The Sonata in C major is cast in "modern" sonata–allegro form with a return of the initial idea. The suave *galant* style probably places it in the 1760s or later. The two minuets are extremely brief, sixteen measures each, with no contrasting trio sections, but they are quite charming.

JUAN SESSÉ (1736–1801) was born in the village of Calanda near Alcañiz. He studied in his native village and in Zaragoza, at first intending to pursue a course in philosophy, but because of difficulty with his eyes, he decided on the profession of organist.

After moving to Madrid, Sessé first held the post of organist at San Felipe de Neri, but eventually became one of the organists at the Royal Chapel. Late in 1768 or at the beginning of 1769, he was appointed third organist, moving to second organist in 1787, a post he held until his death.[40]

Sessé's keyboard works include *Seis fugas para órgano y clave* (1773), *Doce minuetes para clavicordio* (1774), *Ocho divertimentos para clave o forte-piano* (1784), and *Cuaderno tercero de una colección de piezas de música para clavicordio, forte-piano y órgano,* Op. 8.[41]

Many of Sessé's works were published by Copin of Madrid, 1773–1790, but, of the printed editions, apparently only the *Seis fugas para órgano y clave* (1773) has survived.[42] What makes this volume of special interest is that it appears to be the first extant Spanish publication of keyboard music since the 1626 *Facultad Orgánica* by Correa de Arauxo.[43] The six fugues are somewhat "pianistic," as was typical of much of the Spanish organ music of the period, though Sessé's preferred instrument was probably the organ.

FÉLIX MÁXIMO LÓPEZ (1742–1821) began as fourth organist to the Royal Chapel in Madrid in 1775, and by 1805 had been promoted to first organist. He continued in this post until his death. Unfortunately, very little is known about him before his appointment to the Royal Chapel.[44]

The keyboard music of López is preserved in twelve manuscripts at the Biblioteca Nacional in Madrid. Alma Espinosa's exhaustive dissertation (Espinosa/"López") provides a thematic index of the keyboard works as well as an edition of selected works, including sonatas, rondos, *Variaciones al Minuet Afandangado,* and Capricho in E major. Sonata in G minor, a work not included in the Espinosa edition, has been published in Doderer/*Spanische.*

Generally, López's works do not emphasize virtuosity. However, some works do contain wide leaps, repeated-note figures, octaves, and hand-crossings similar to those in many of the works of Scarlatti and Soler. See Ex. 14 from *Música de clave.* But these technical problems are seldom as difficult as those found in the sonatas of López's famed predecessors.

López's sonatas are all multi-movement works and in the *galant* style of the mid-eighteenth century, though the composer lived into the early nineteenth century. Ex. 15, from the opening of the finale in Sonata in C major (*Música de clave,* Espinosa edition), shows the *fácil y buen gusto* of this style with its two- to three-voice texture, "singing" melody, and simple accompaniment.

Ex. 14. López, *Pieza de clave in D major*/13–46. © 1976 Alma Espinosa. Used by permission.

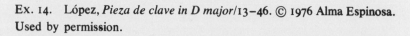

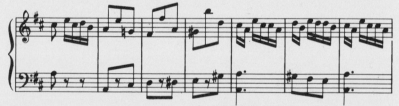

Ex. 15.   López, Sonata in C major/iv/1–11. © 1976 Alma Espinosa. Used by permission.

The title *Variaciones al Minuet Afandangado* suggests the influence of the *fandango,* but in López's composition no such influence is apparent. This form usually employs quick changes between relative major and minor keys and certain recognizable rhythmic patterns, as can be found in Soler's *Fandango* for keyboard. The López work shows neither the harmonic nor the rhythmic characteristics of the typical Spanish *fandango.* Occasionally, however, when this dance is used in art music, some of these characteristics are lost. Perhaps López was following the example of Gluck (*Don Juan*) and Mozart (*Figaro*) by using a preexistent melody.[45]

Of his total output for keyboard, Espinosa finds the sonatas the most interesting. She states that "his use of a clear articulation at the beginning of the recapitulation marks him as one of the most progressive Spanish composers of his generation."[46] John Gillespie goes a step further in saying that the finest sonatas by López are the two in C major written for four hands.[47]

Although the sonatas come from a manuscript entitled *Música de clave* ("Music for Harpsichord"), they are definitely styled for piano technique and even contain expression markings commonly associated with the piano. Undoubtedly, they were intended for piano or harpsichord—whichever was available.

JOSÉ LIDÓN (1746–1827) was born in Béjar, Salamanca.[48] He became organist at the Royal Chapel in Madrid in 1768 and served in that position for 37 years, until 1805, when he became chapelmaster there and rector of the king's Real Colegio de Niños Cantores.

Keyboard works by Lidón include *Seis piezas o sonatas para órgano* and *Seis fugas* (1792).[49] Nin mentions a treatise by Lidón entitled *Règles pour les organistes et les amateurs de piano* (1775), but does not speak very highly of it, stating that it is simply a manual about accompaniment.[50]

Thus far, only one work by Lidón has been made available (other than organ works such as *intentos*)—*Sonata de 1° tono para clave o para órgano con trompeta real*.[51] Kastner points out that on the title page of a 1787 publication, Lidón calls himself "Master of the Italian Style at the Royal College."[52] Although we cannot verify this claim from the single sonata available for inspection, Newman calls this work "a tightly knit, harmonically strong piece in binary design that whets the appetite for more in spite of its conservative, motivic style and close resemblance to many of the shorter, more concentrated pieces of Scarlatti."[53]

JOAQUÍN TADEO MURGUÍA (1758–1836), originally of Basque origin, became organist of the Cathedral of Málaga. He was noted for his ability to improvise at the organ, and, according to Rafaël Mitjana, wrote *Sonates pour piano*, for four hands.[54] Murguía's works are in MS in the archives of the Cathedral of Málaga.

Seville and the Basque Region

Two very important but little known Spanish composers of harpsichord and piano music in the late eighteenth century were MANUEL BLASCO DE NEBRA (1750–1784) and JOAQUÍN MONTERO (c.1764–c.1815). They are mentioned jointly because they both worked in Seville and both wrote collections of keyboard music entitled *Seis sonatas para clave y fuerte piano* ("Six Sonatas for Harpsichord and Piano"), thus providing a good basis for comparison.

The Library of Congress possesses what is apparently the sole copy of the eighteenth-century edition of the Blasco de Nebra sonatas.[55] These six sonatas, listed as Op. 1, are the only known extant pieces by Blasco de Nebra. According to the Library of Congress, they were published in 1780 in Madrid. The library of the Orfeó Català in Barcelona owns what is possibly the only surviving eighteenth-century edition of the Montero sonatas, also listed as Op. 1. They, too, were published in Madrid, but ten years later, in 1790. Baciero/Nueva biblioteca III:ix-x mentions that five of the Blasco de Nebra sonatas can be found in a MS in the archives of the Cathedral of Valladolid.

Little biographical information is available about Blasco de Nebra except that he was a pupil of his uncle José de Nebra and that he was organist at the Cathedral in Seville. Several sources indicate his tenure there as 1750 to 1784.[56] But these dates are in fact his birth and death dates, announced in the *Gaceta de Madrid,* December 30, 1785.[57] This periodical also states that he composed 172 works.

Information on Joaquín Montero also is woefully lacking. Baltasar Saldoni indicates that he was organist of the parish church of San Pedro el Real in Seville in the second half of the eighteenth century.[58] In addition to the six sonatas, Montero published a *Compendio armónico* in 1790; some sonatas and minuets in 1796; and another treatise, *Tratado teórico-práctico sobre el con-*

trapunto, dated 1815, a copy of which is available in the Biblioteca Capitular y Colombina of Seville and in the Biblioteca de Catalunya in Barcelona.

From a dated manuscript in the Biblioteca Nacional in Madrid, we can assume that Montero was active as a composer as early as 1764. Halfway through the manuscript, which is entitled *Joan Roig y Posas, Comercian en Barcelona 1764,* we read: *Síguese 12 Minuetes para Clave y Piano Fuerte, compuestos por D. Joaquin Montero* ("Following Are 12 Minuets for Harpsichord and Piano, composed by D. Joaquin Montero"). Actually there are only ten minuets in this group. They are very concise, contain no contrasting trio sections, and possess a great deal of charm.[59] But what is more important, they represent some of the earliest Spanish keyboard works that specifically indicate the piano in the title.[60]

Only a few years later, in 1780, Blasco de Nebra's *Seis sonatas para clave y fuerte piano,* Op. 1, appeared. They contain no

> dynamic or other editorial markings except for minimal tempo indications, but the use of the piano is made likely by long tones that must be sustained in order to project songful lines (Sonata No. 5/i), by searching, dissonant harmony that seems to call for the most subtle nuances (Sonata No. 1/i), by rapid passages in octaves for each hand (Sonatas No. 4/ii and No. 2/ii), and by ever-changing textures.[61]

In 1780, the fact that the range of the sonatas exceeds five octaves would not necessarily point to any one instrument. But, by the time of Montero's *Seis sonatas para clave y fuerte piano,* Op. 1, of 1790, there is no doubt that the piano is the preferred instrument, for there are numerous indications of *piano* and *forte* as well as signs for *crescendo* and *decrescendo.*

The most obvious similarity between the Blasco de Nebra sonatas and the Montero sonatas is that both collections contain six sonatas, each in two movements of contrasting tempos: a slow movement paired with a faster movement. (As we have observed with Scarlatti and Soler, the pairing of sonatas was not uncommon in Spain at this time.) In both sets of sonatas, each movement employs the usual binary design with repeated halves. Nine of the twelve movements of Blasco de Nebra's sonatas exhibit embryonic sonata–allegro form. Only one movement is closer to the Scarlattian type of sonata.

Both Blasco de Nebra and Montero display well-defined syntax in the phrase structure of their sonatas, this characteristic placing them closer to Haydn and Mozart than to Scarlatti, but in their persistence of repetition of short musical ideas, they are more similar to Scarlatti. However, their motives are more likely than Scarlatti's to be extended into complete themes. In Ex. 16, from Blasco de Nebra's Sonata No. 3/i, note the pungent Scarlattian appoggiaturas within the clear phrase structure. Compare that passage with Ex. 17 from Montero's Sonata No. 1/i, which is decidedly more akin to the *style galant,* with its series of restless, short-winded clauses marked off by rests.

Ex. 16.   Blasco de Nebra, Sonata No. 3/i/7–15. © 1964. Used by permission of the publisher, Union Musical Española.

Ex. 17. Montero, Sonata No. 1/i/1–12. © 1977. Used by permission of the publisher, Union Musical Española.

Both composers wrote in an idiomatic style for the keyboard. It is remarkable, particularly for two Spanish composers following Scarlatti, that their sonatas do not contain hand-crossings. The chief difficulty in the right hand in the Blasco de Nebra sonatas, beyond the usual requirements of broken-chord figures and scalar passages, is the playing of broken octaves and tenths in figuration. Ex. 18, from Sonata No. 5/ii, shows Blasco de Nebra's striking use of leaping tenths in both hands. One of the most difficult passages in the Montero sonatas occurs in Sonata No. 5/ii. The movement is marked *presto* and involves two measures of broken thirds followed by two measures of harmonic thirds in the right hand, reminding one of Clementi. See Ex. 19.

Ex. 18. Blasco de Nebra, Sonata No. 5/ii/141–148. © 1964. Used by permission of the publisher, Union Musical Española.

Ex. 19. Montero, Sonata No. 5/ii/12–19. © 1977. Used by permission of the publisher, Union Musical Española.

Concerning accompaniment figures, the use of the Alberti bass is notably absent from the Blasco de Nebra sonatas, but is distinctively present in the Montero sonatas. This one stylistic feature figures prominently in contrasting the two composers. However, Blasco de Nebra comes closest to the "Classic" spirit in the last movement of Sonata No. 6, where he uses an oscillating accompaniment to set off a Haydnesque melody (see Ex. 20). Compare that with a similar spirit in the excerpt from Montero's Sonata No. 2/ii, in which there is a true Alberti bass pattern (Ex. 21).

Ex. 20.   Blasco de Nebra, Sonata No. 6/ii/149–156. © 1964. Used by permission of the publisher, Union Musical Española.

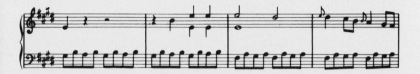

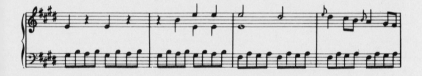

Ex. 21.   Montero, Sonata No. 2/ii/32–38. © 1977. Used by permission of the publisher, Union Musical Española.

Another stylistic distinction between the two Spaniards can be seen in Blasco de Nebra's telling use of guitar effects, for example, the *rasgueado*, or strummed-chord technique. Kirkpatrick describes this effect, which appears quite often in Scarlatti's sonatas, as "savage chords that at times almost threaten to rip the strings from the instrument."[62] Note that this seems to be the intention of Blasco de Nebra in Sonata No. 3/ii (see Ex. 22). We cannot consider his use of this effect unusual since he worked in Seville, the very heart of Andalusia. One other harmonic trait of Blasco de Nebra that shows the influence of Scarlatti is the presence of *acciaccatura* chords (Sonata No. 5/ii). Joaquin Montero, composing in the more cosmopolitan style a bit later, was not at all interested in transferring guitar effects to the keyboard, though he too worked in Seville, or in writing such biting dissonances as those found in the Scarlattian *acciaccatura* chords.

Ex. 22.   Blasco de Nebra, Sonata No. 3/ii/61–72. © 1964. Used by permission of the publisher, Union Musical Española.

Newman describes Blasco de Nebra aptly when he states,

> insofar as his one youthful set of sonatas permits us to know
> him, [he] seems to be the peer of Scarlatti and Soler in original-
> ity, force and depth of expression. His language, for the most
> part, is no closer than Soler's to that of the high Classic masters.
> In fact, his penetrating, sometimes anguished dissonances,
> suggest the earlier 18th century.[63]

Montero, however, was more influenced by the universal language
of the high Classic masters. Almost all the movements of his
sonatas approximate sonata–allegro form and show a very lucid
melodic organization, which often reveals a balance of antecedent
and consequent phrases. Alberti bass or similar accompaniment
patterns help to create motion and provide a backdrop for his many
songful melodies. Although it cannot be said that Montero was the
peer of Haydn or Mozart, he left us some delightful sonatas in his
first published opus.

As a result of the publication of anthologies by José Antonio
Donostía and Antonio Ruiz-Pipó, we are able to investigate more
thoroughly keyboard music from the Basque region of Spain.[64]
Ruiz-Pipó's edition, *Música vasca del siglo XVIII para tecla,* offers
a sampling of Basque keyboard music taken mostly from the
monastery of Aránzazu, a cloister not as well known as Montserrat
or the Escorial.

At the monastery of Aránzazu, there is known to have been an
organ, a harpsichord, several Spanish oboes (flageolets), bassoons,
and a children's choir, but no piano.[65] Again, the accessibility of
the organ proves significant. Moreover, many of the composers
were organists/priests, but they too were aware of the ever-
changing styles from across the Pyrenees and tended to compose
accordingly.

JOSÉ LARRAÑAGA (c.1730–1806) was a Franciscan monk and
chapelmaster at Aránzazu. Evidently he was quite knowledgeable
about organs, since in 1789 he was engaged as a technical expert
for the planned organ in the parish of Tolosa.

Ruiz-Pipó has published four sonatas and a work entitled *La Valenciana* by Larrañaga in his edition. Larrañaga employs full sonata–allegro form in two works (Sonatas in D major and G major) and the Scarlatti-type design in the other two (Sonatas in C major and D minor). Sonata in C major, like some sonatas we shall encounter by the Catalan Baguer, possesses a symphonic style reminiscent of early Haydn, while Sonata in D major contains a touch of the Spanish folk element. Sonata in D minor is the most appealing work of the lot, nearer to Scarlatti than the rest. Note the wailing appoggiaturas and guitar effects in Ex. 23.

Ex. 23.   Larrañaga, Sonata in D minor/11–16. © 1972. Used by permission of the publisher, Union Musical Española.

MANUEL DE GAMMARA (active 1772–1786) was chapelmaster of the Real Sociedad Vascongada in Victoria. The only other information known about him is that he wrote an opera called *El médico avariento* (1772). Only two of his keyboard works appear in *Música vasca,* a brief *Verso* in C major and Sonata in A minor. Apparently he wrote other sonatas, but they have been lost. Sonata in A minor opens in Vivaldi fashion, with steady driving Baroque pulse, but soon lapses into a more pre-Classic style. The design is binary with no recapitulation of the opening theme.

FERNANDO EGUIGUREN (b.1743) was born in Eibar and became a priest at Aránzazu in 1759. The solitary keyboard work known by this Basque composer is entitled *Concierto Airoso,* though it resembles a sonata in binary form. The *Concierto* exhibits a symphonic martial opening with many figures common to the string section of a Classical work. Unusual is the fact that Eguiguren introduces a new lyrical theme at the point where the recapitulation is expected.

Padre ANDRES LONBIDE (b.1745) of Elgueta, Guipúzcoa, became organist of the parish of Santiago in Bilbao. Of his musical activities, we know that he wrote a treatise entitled *El arte de organista* and *Seis sonatas para clave y violín,* now lost. His keyboard work in the Ruiz-Pipó edition, the single-movement Sonata in D major, displays a binary design with no recapitulation of the initial idea. This work in 6/8 features a general symphonic style with oscillating patterns in the accompaniment and a somewhat unfocused harmonic style that lacks good tonal direction.

Of Padre AGUSTÍN ECHEVERRÍA (d.1792) we know only that he died at Aránzazu, where there are preserved sacred works dated 1756 to 1791. The one-movement Sonata in E-flat major by Echeverría (from *Música vasca*) has a return to the opening theme in the tonic, thus showing his awareness of mature sonata–allegro form. It is simply constructed from incessant repetitions of ideas with no motivic development, a trait found all too often in Spanish keyboard music of the period.

MANUEL DE SOSTOA (b.1749), from the town of Eibar, became a priest at Aránzazu in 1764. He was supposedly an outstanding composer of sacred works. Preserved at the monastery are works by Sostoa dated 1768, 1801, and 1802.[66] Only one work, *Allegro* in D major, has been published in Ruiz-Pipó's anthology. Despite its title, it manifests the characteristics of a sonata, complete with binary form and return of the opening theme in the second half. With all its simplicity, this small work has more immediate appeal than many of the Basque compositions thus far available for study. Its melodic charm, logical accompaniments, and Spanish folk influence all add to its attractiveness.

Three other composers who worked in and about the Basque region must be considered here. Of JOSÉ FERRER (active 1780–1781), it is known only that he was organist at the Cathedral of Pamplona and that in 1780 he published in Madrid *Seis sonatas para forte piano ó clavicordio,* followed in 1781 by *Tres sonatas para clave y forte piano con acompañamiento de violín.*[67] So far, none of these works have been rediscovered, but a miscellaneous manuscript at the Biblioteca de Catalunya in Barcelona contains two sonatas by José Ferrer.[68]

MATEO PÉREZ DE ALBÉNIZ (d.1831), father of Pedro Albéniz (1795–1855), was a noted chapelmaster in Logroño and San Sebastián. According to Nin and Saldoni, he enjoyed the greatest esteem among his contemporaries.[69] Only one sonata of his is known, Sonata in D major, with lively patterns in 6/8, probably a *zapateado.*[70] The binary design, complete with crux, recalls Scarlatti, but the hammer-stroke cadences and phrase syntax betray a later generation.

JULIÁN PRIETO (1765–1844), of Santo Domingo de la Calzada, studied composition in Zaragoza with Xavier García and was known to have had a beautiful tenor voice. Later, he became the organist at the Cathedral of Pamplona. According to François-Joseph Fétis, the noted French music historian of the nineteenth century, he wrote melodies of "good taste and of grace."[71]

Sonata in C major in three movements by Prieto has been published in Baciero/*Nueva biblioteca* I.[72] The first movement has a binary structure with no recapitulation of the main theme. Again we see that the Scarlatti-type design has penetrated all regions of Spain. However, the style is *galant,* with triplet patterns for accompaniment. The second movement, *Andante con espresione,* is unusually short, only sixteen measures. The rondo finale proves to be the most attractive movement of the sonata, with its energetic right-hand sextuplet figures and Mozartean trills on the supertonic and leading tone driving to the cadence.

Montserrat, Barcelona, and Related Posts

Padre ANSELMO VIOLA (1738–1798) was born in Torruela, Gerona, and was educated at the famed monastery of Montserrat, where he eventually became chapelmaster.

Thirteen manuscript sonatas for organ or harpsichord by Viola are preserved at Montserrat.[73] One of these, Sonata in D major, published in Doderer/*Spanische,* opens with strokes of tonic and dominant and a texture more akin to many sinfonias of the period (see Ex. 24). The gay festive mood also characterizes the second theme, which features a two-voice texture and horn fifths. The most striking aspect of the work is the startling excursion to C-sharp minor in the development section that leads to a recapitulation in the dominant. Fétis even notes Viola's bold modulations.[74]

Ex. 24.   Viola, Sonata in D major/1–8. Copyright © 1975 Willy Mueller, Sueddeutscher Musikverlag, Heidelberg. Used by permission of C.F. Peters Corporation, New York.

Padre NARCISO CASANOVAS (1747–1799), of Sabadell near Barcelona, received his training at the Escolania of Montserrat and became one of the most celebrated composers and organists at Montserrat. Saldoni attests to his ability as a performer:

Padre Casanovas was one of the better, if not the best organist of his epoch; according to those who heard him, he had no rival. Peculiarly, his fingers were so big that with the tips of them he covered the keyboard completely and no one understood how he played so cleanly and with such surprising execution, without stumbling on the other keys, because the width of the keys had very little space for each finger.[75]

Twenty-four sonatas by Casanovas are extant, three of which are entitled *Sonata per clarins*.[76] Eight of the keyboard sonatas plus a Rondo have been issued in a modern edition.[77] Five of them show a more mature sonata–allegro form with recapitulations of the main thematic material; while the other three are more of the Scarlatti type, with parallel thematic return near the end of each half of the binary designs.

Sonata in A major (No. 1 in the Pujol edition) is one of Casanovas' most attractive works in print (see Ex. 25). It has an Italianate sparkle and features very idiomatic writing for the keyboard.

Ex. 25. Casanovas, Sonata in A major/1–14. © 1934 Publicacions de l'Abadia de Monserrat. Used by permission.

Although FELIPE RODRÍGUEZ (1759–1814) was born in Madrid, he became a monk and organist at Montserrat. Later he returned to Madrid to serve in the affiliated Montserrat church.

The music archives at Montserrat preserve a manuscript collection that includes eighteen sonatas in one to three movements and sixteen rondos by F. Rodríguez. The sonatas are designated for organ, but here again we encounter a Spanish organist writing in a style featuring Alberti basses and other light chordal accompaniments, a style more associated with the piano by the late eighteenth century.

Fifteen of the sonatas and Rondo in B-flat major are available in modern edition.[78] The Rondo is indeed a captivating, light, playful work with many aviary trills that almost seem to "twitter" and "chirp." Of the sonatas in print, thirteen movements contain binary structures with no recapitulations, while nine exhibit a more mature sonata–allegro form. All the three-movement sonatas and two of the two-movement sonatas end with rondos.

One of the most attractive stylistic characteristics of F. Rodríguez is the folk-dance atmosphere he creates with a guitarlike figure featuring an internal pedal point (see Ex. 26). Very often these passages prove to be the most interesting sections of the works.

Ex. 26.   F. Rodríguez, Sonata in F minor/i/47–54. © 1936 Publicacions de l'Abadia de Montserrat. Used by permission.

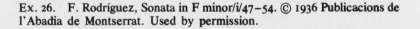

JOSEP VINYALS (1771–1825), of Terrassa, near Barcelona, studied at Montserrat and at age nineteen joined the monastic order there. He also became one of the many organists of the famous monastery.

At age sixteen Vinyals composed five sonatas *Para diversión del Sr. D. Infante,* but the identity of the *Infante* is not known. A more mature Sonata in E-flat major has been published in modern edition.[79] It is in two movements, a *presto* in complete sonata–allegro form and a Rondo, Tempo di Menuetto. The first movement appears more satisfactory than many works by Vinyals' Spanish contemporaries. In appraising this sonata, Newman says, "Vinyals uses fewer ideas, makes more of them and organizes them into simpler, broader forms."[80]

FREIXANET (born c.1730) was most likely a Catalan composer. No information about him is available, not even concerning his name. Three sonatas by Freixanet have been published in modern editions—Sonata in G major and Sonata in A major,[81] and Sonata in B-flat major.[82]

Sonata in G major is of the Scarlatti type with crux, while Sonata in A major shows signs of early sonata–allegro form with full recapitulation and two major themes. Sonata in B-flat major bears resemblance to sonata–allegro form but with only partial recapitulation. The opening of the main theme does not recur, but the subsequent phrase does return in the tonic key.

All three sonatas show the influence of the *galant* style— frequent series of triplets, appoggiatura "sighs," "Scotch snaps" (Lombard rhythm), general two-voice texture.[83] Ex. 27 illustrates many of these salient features, which were common to Spanish composers as well as to the whole of Europe in this period.

Of the composer CANTALLOS (c.1760), nothing is known, not even his complete name. One work has been attributed to him, an attractive Sonata in C minor, which has been published in Nin/ *Classiques* I and in Marchi/*Clavicembalisti.*[84]

Sonata in C minor is of the Scarlatti type, complete with crux. According to Nin, it recalls the *zapateado,* with a stirring synco-

Ex. 27.   Freixanet, Sonata in G major/51–62. © 1929. Used by permission of the publisher, Editions Max Eschig.

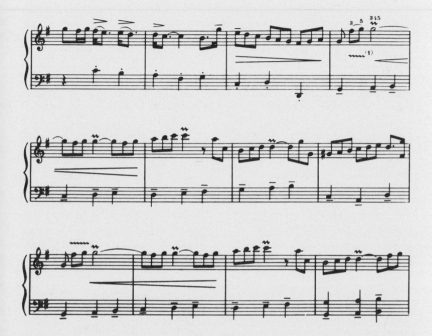

pated conclusion to both halves of the bipartite design. Notable also is the remote modulation to G-sharp minor in the second half of the work. Of this striking work, Newman goes so far as to say it "is an effective piece, with more textural and thematic fiber, more tonal and keyboard enterprise. . . ."[85]

BLAS SERRANO (c.1770) is yet another Spanish composer about whom we know virtually nothing. Only one solitary Sonata in B-flat major gives evidence of his existence.[86] This one-movement sonata is "a delightful Italian aria, full of charm, elegance and tenderness."[87] It proves to be more "modern" for its time than the work by Cantallos, or, as Newman states, "decidedly more advanced in style and syntax, suggesting the homophony and cantabile themes of Christian Bach in spite of its surfeit of short trills.''[88] This work indeed attests to the fact that Spanish styles did not lag far behind the rest of the continent at that time.

JUAN MORENO Y POLO (active 1754–1776) was organist at the Cathedral of Tortosa, province of Tarragona. The only other information we have about him is that he wrote ''Sonatines'' described as charming and advanced for their time.[89] His brother JOSÉ MORENO Y POLO (d.1773) was born in La Hoz, Aragón, and died in Madrid. José studied in Zaragoza and was appointed second organist of the Basílica del Pilar. Later he became first organist of the Cathedral of Albarracín, Teruel, where he entered the priesthood. Among his works there are supposedly 100 sonatas in manuscript.[90]

JOSÉ GALLÉS (1761–1836), a Catalan monk and organist born in Castelltersol, served as chapelmaster at the Cathedral of Vich north of Barcelona. Gallés' extant keyboard works are preserved in a manuscript volume in the Biblioteca de Catalunya of Barcelona. The collection contains 23 sonatas, six of which are published in modern edition.[91]

All 23 of the Gallés sonatas are in the traditional binary form, but it is noteworthy that only three (Nos. 20, 21, and 22) are cast in the more ''modern'' sonata form (with recapitulation of the first theme), and that they are among the last in the manuscript collection. Six (Nos. 4, 17, 19, 21, 22, and 23, as numbered in the MS) have major cadences marked with fermatas and the term *arbitrio*, indicating a free elaboration or short cadenza at this point in the work (see Ex. 28). This term was also used in some of the sonatas of Felipe Rodríguez, Josep Vinyals, and Anselmo Viola.

Ex. 28.   Gallés, Sonata in C minor/25–29. © 1955. Used by permission of the publisher, G. Ricordi & c.s.p.a., Milan.

Although the style of Gallés is essentially rooted in the Classical idiom, he does not let us forget that he is a Spanish composer, employing colorful folklike material in his sonatas; e.g., in Nin/ *Classiques* II, the Sonatas in A-flat major, B minor, B-flat major, C major, and C minor (see Ex. 29). The most appealing work of the group is Sonata in F minor (No. 17 in Nin/*Classiques* II and No. 8 in Marchi/*Clavicembalisti*), a "toccata" type with driving figurations, close finger work, and hand-crossings. Noticeable here is the excursion into A-flat minor in the second half, climaxing with a German augmented-sixth chord.

Ex. 29. Gallés, Sonata in B-flat major/17–24. © 1929. Used by permission of the publisher, Editions Max Eschig.

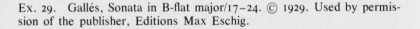

Although there are many exciting and colorful passages in the Gallés sonatas, they suffer from a symptom often found in works by a number of his Spanish contemporaries—incessant repetition. According to Newman's exhaustive study of the sonata idea, instead of motivic working-out, many Spanish sonatas of this period simply contain melodic fragments that are merely repeated until the repetitions or slight alterations thereof add up to the phrases and periods needed to fill out a section.[92]

CARLOS BAGUER (1768–1808) of Barcelona became organist of the cathedral in his native city. Very little is known of his life except that he composed operas, oratorios, and motets, as well as works for the keyboard. Some of his keyboard works, all in manuscript, can be found in the Biblioteca de Catalunya and the library of the Orfeó Català in Barcelona. The manuscript at the Orfeó Català is entitled *Sonatas de Pᵉ Fray Antonio Soler que hizo para la diversion del Serenissimo Señor Infante Don Gabriel, Obra 1ᵃ y 8ᵃ, Año 1786, Joseph Antonio Terrés, 1802*. Included in this collection of Soler sonatas are six sonatas and four rondos by Carlos Baguer.

All the sonatas are in single movements in binary design and exhibit mature sonata–allegro form except the first one, in F major. This piece is more akin to the Scarlatti sonata, with parallel thematic return near the end of each half. Nevertheless, the style is more the cosmopolitan language of the generation of Haydn and Mozart than that of Scarlatti.

The texture of the sonatas is often more symphonic than keyboard-oriented; for example, the bold opening in octaves of Sonata in G major, with a sudden contrast as if scored for woodwinds; and the opening of Sonata in B-flat major, with its horn fifths in the left hand and string tremolo effects in the right hand.

Regarding Baguer's harmony, two passages stand out in the sonatas above all others. Just before the arrival of the second theme in the Sonata in G major (mm. 24–25), two different augmented-sixth chords are introduced at the cadence on the dominant of the dominant. The first altered chord, spelled F–A –D-sharp (F–A–E-flat), resolves as a dominant to its fifth-related chord of B-flat, which in turn becomes B-flat–D–F–G-sharp and resolves finally to the dominant of the dominant (see Ex. 30). The other passage occurs in Sonata in B-flat major, where Baguer begins the second theme in the key of D-flat major instead of the traditional F major, with a resulting tertian relationship.

Neither the sonatas nor the short, superficial rondos by Baguer are profound pieces for keyboard when compared to similar works

Ex. 30.   Baguer, Sonata in G Major/22–27.

of the time by Haydn or Mozart. Nonetheless, they exhibit attempts by a little-known Spanish composer to keep abreast of the times, during an age when Italian vocal music was steadily mounting in popularity in Spain.

MATEO FERRER (1788–1864), a student of Francisco Queralt, was one of the most outstanding musicians from Barcelona in the first half of the nineteenth century. He studied organ, piano, contrabass, and flute. In 1808, at age 20, he succeeded Baguer as organist of the Cathedral in Barcelona, a position he held for 56 years. In 1830 he was also named *maestro de capilla* of the cathedral. M. Ferrer even eventually replaced the famous Ramón Carnicer as maestro of the theater of Santa Cruz.[93]

Unfortunately, only one keyboard work by M. Ferrer is available for study, Sonata in D major, published in Nin/*Classiques* I. Nin gives no details of the manuscript source other than he had a "very old copy" and that this work is the first movement of a "grande sonate."[94]

Although M. Ferrer lived well into the Romantic period, his Sonata in D major demonstrates his preference for the Classical style. This work is in mature sonata–allegro form. It opens in symphonic style with a rocket figure reminiscent of the Mannheim school. Probably its most striking aspect is a beautiful deceptive cadence that uses the lowered sixth scale degree in the second theme. This composition inspires hopes that more works by M. Ferrer will soon be discovered.

Summary

The Italian Domenico Scarlatti had by far the most influence on Spanish keyboard composers of the eighteenth century. The style and form of a typical Scarlatti sonata was emulated by numerous Spanish composers of that period, with a gradual shift to the newer trends of Haydn.

Although Scarlatti's sonatas, at the hands of a good performer, can be effective on the piano, they truly come to life with the bite of a plucked stringed keyboard instrument. Because of problems of range and lack of brilliance, Scarlatti most likely preferred the harpsichord to the newer pianofortes at the Spanish courts.

Scarlatti composed some of the most difficult music ever written for harpsichord, though much of it is in a highly idiomatic manner. His keyboard style is characterized by brilliant figurations, arpeggios, wide leaps, rapid repeated notes, and hand-crossings. He wrote many colorful works that suggest various timbres, e.g., fanfare trumpets, flutes, bagpipes, and the ever-present guitar, which he emulated melodically as well as harmonically. No less appealing are his many sonatas that were influenced by Spanish folk music. In certain works, he uses obvious material from the *saeta, bulerías, peteneras,* and *jota.*

The influence of Scarlatti on native Spanish composers is especially noteworthy in the works of the Valencian Vicente Rodríguez, the first native Spaniard to write sonatas (1744); Sebastián de Albero, who was possibly the first Spaniard to use "pianoforte" in the title of a keyboard collection, perhaps as early as 1746; Antonio Soler, the single most important disciple of Scarlatti and a composer of great stature in his own right; Manuel Blasco de Nebra, who worked in Seville and who left us some extraordinary works with a mixture of eighteenth-century styles; and José Larrañaga, of Basque origin, who shows that he was equally at home with the Scarlatti style and the more *galant* trend. Though the Catalan composers often used a form similar to that of many of Scarlatti's sonatas, they more often steered away from the basic procedures associated with Scarlatti, choosing instead the mid-century style in addition to a bit of local color.

Since the terms *clavicordio, clave, órgano, címbalo (clavecímbalo),* and *pianoforte (fuerte piano)* were all used in Spanish keyboard music of the eighteenth century, one must approach the matter of "the correct instrument to be employed" with some flexibility. Some works indicate *para clavicordio o piano forte* and others *para clave y fuerte piano* or *para órgano y clave*. Spanish keyboard works with contents similar to that of Scarlatti's sonatas sound best on the harpsichord, of course. However, many of the Spanish organists/priests no doubt performed their works, regardless of style, on the instrument most available to them, the organ. Those works of a *galant* character seem more desirable today on a stringed keyboard instrument, especially a replica of an eighteenth-century pianoforte.

One curious aspect regarding terminology is Albero's use of the term *clavicordio* instead of *clave* or *címbalo* in his *Obras para clavicordio o piano forte* and *Sonatas para clavicordio*. One wonders if he specifically intended the clavichord or was using the term in a general sense to indicate harpsichord or clavichord. Antonio Baciero, in the preface to his edition of Albero's *Sonatas para clavicordio,* vol. I, contends that Albero's use of the term *clavicordio* should be treated the same as Scarlatti's indication for harpsichord *(cembalo)* and that our term for clavichord today was indicated in Spain traditionally by the term *monacordio*.

One aspect that, in many cases, sets eighteenth-century Spanish keyboard music apart from other European keyboard music of the period is its use of regional or folk material. As we have already noted, Scarlatti employed guitar effects as well as actual Spanish folk rhythms in his sonatas. This practice was followed especially by Albero, Soler, Blasco de Nebra, Larrañaga, F. Rodríguez, and José Gallés. Following a more universal trend, Montero (Seville), Prieto (Navarra), Freixanet (Catalonia), and M. Ferrer (Catalonia) wrote works that sound as if they might have been written by any European composer of the late eighteenth or early nineteenth century. The Catalan composers Viola and Baguer, as well as the Basque composers Larrañaga, Eguiguren, and Lonbide, even wrote keyboard works in a *galant* style that are symphonic in nature and reminiscent of the Mannheim school.

CHAPTER TWO

The Piano Music of Isaac Albéniz, Enrique Granados, Their Immediate Predecessors, and Their Contemporaries

Introduction

The first part of the nineteenth century was a time of turmoil for Spain. By 1808, 100,000 of Napoleon's soldiers occupied Spanish territory. For a while the throne was in doubt, Charles IV having abdicated in the same year. Fernando VII claimed the throne, but under pressure from Napoleon, renounced the crown to his brother Joseph, king of Naples. The Spaniards refused to accept the imposition of a foreign ruler and declared war on France.

The period was indeed one of economic and political stagnation for Spain. However, two important figures came out of this upheaval—the older a painter, the younger a musician. The first was Francisco Goya (1746–1828), who left us some lasting impressions of the horrors of war in Spain in 1808: a set of drawings called *Disasters of War* and the famous painting *May 3, 1808,* which portrays the execution of Spanish loyalists at the hands of the French. The other was Juan Crisóstomo de Arriaga (1806–1826), one of Spain's most important composers of chamber music; unfortunately, his untimely death left the nation without a major composer in the first half of the nineteenth century.

Fernando VII returned to Spain in 1814, ignored the Constitution of 1812, and restored absolute rule. However, harsh treatment of the liberals and his capricious administration soon provoked a revolt. Military officers, together with the liberals, forced Fernando to restore the Constitution in 1820. For three years, the country was in yet another state of agitation. The liberals split into moderate and extreme factions, and the royalists continued to plot against them. Meanwhile, the other European powers decided to intervene. A French force invaded Spain in 1823, rescuing Fernando VII from virtual imprisonment. Although the French had hoped that the king would introduce moderate constitutional rule, he returned to his earlier repressive policies against the liberals, policies he carried to the grave.

Isabel II, the three-year-old daughter of Fernando VII, was proclaimed queen in 1833, and her mother, María Cristina, was named regent. Many opposed this succession, in favor of Don Carlos, brother of Fernando VII. The Carlist wars ensued and lasted six years. Isabel's reign ended in 1868, when the Republic was proclaimed.

The general musical scene was in a deplorable state. As Nin writes:

> With [Mateo] Ferrer (1788–1864) we are in the very middle of national degeneration. Phillipe V's policy of annihilation had borne its fruits [regarding his preference for Italian over native musicians]. Spanish music, which had held on to the end of the eighteenth century behind the rampart of the tonadilla, the last refuge of the nationalist musicians, was completely lethargic. The opera, [that] incurable soreness of Spain, had to be Italian or it could not be. The devotees of chamber music revolved around Luigi Boccherini. The old-timers were talking about Haydn, who had been one of the musical idols of Spain, as an outmoded memory. One forgets ancestors, one disregards the past. One marks time where he is or goes forward without purpose, at random. Bellini, Mercadante, Donizetti, Rossini, Verdi reign as absolute masters, one after the other. Italian becomes the one and only approved and possible language. One speaks of nothing but opera all day and all night. At every street corner one hears someone humming, whistling, singing, "howling" the

same old sentimental threadbare lyrics. The high-tenor is adored like the "torero," and the "diva" is enthroned with as much haughtiness as stupidity.[1]

In light of the political and musical situation, it is not surprising to find that no Spanish masterworks for piano were written in the first half of the nineteenth century. It was generally a time of light salon music, bombastic fantasias on operatic themes, or meager attempts to continue the *style galant*. However, during the last decades of the century and the early part of the twentieth century, Isaac Albéniz and Enrique Granados ushered in a keyboard renaissance that resulted in Spain's golden age of piano music. They instigated a rebirth of nationalism, aided by such important pioneers of Spanish nationalism as Felipe Pedrell and Federico Olmeda, both of whom helped to free Spanish music from the dominance of Italianism.

Immediate Predecessors and Contemporaries

JUAN CRISÓSTOMO DE ARRIAGA (1806–1826) of Bilbao, one of the brightest stars on the Spanish horizon, died ten days before his twentieth birthday. With his death, as with those of Albero and Blasco de Nebra in the eighteenth century, Spain lost yet another promising composer at a very early age.

Arriaga wrote an opera at the age of thirteen, even before he had had formal lessons in harmony. In 1821 he was sent to study at the Paris Conservatory, where he received instruction on the violin from Baillot and studied harmony with François-Joseph Fétis. Within two years he impressed Cherubini with his contrapuntal facility, and eventually he was named an auxiliary professor at the conservatory.

Arriaga's compositional style is essentially rooted in the Classical idiom. He has even been called "the Spanish Mozart," and his three string quartets certainly make him the peer of Haydn. However, his only three works for piano do not approach the excellence of his string music nor do they reflect the language of the high Classic masters. They form a part of the new literature for the piano in the early nineteenth century—the character piece, or Romantic miniature—as is evident from their title, *Estudios o Caprichos (Estudios de carácter).*[2]

The three works in the collection, *Allegro, Moderato,* and *Risoluto,* reflect the early German Romantic styles of Schubert, Schumann, and Mendelssohn, respectively, though it was probably too early for these composers to have influenced Arriaga directly. In the first of the *Estudios* the two main themes are similar. They are based on an arpeggiated figure and organized within the sonata principle. Certain harmonic elements remind one of Schubert. The second selection contains an incessant rhythmic figure repeated through various keys with striking modulations (see Ex. 1), and resembles one of Schumann's *Novellettes.* The final piece, which is perhaps the most appealing, reflects the "elfin" music of Mendelssohn in 6/8. Its *perpetuum mobile* activity is organized in sonata form.

Ex. 1. Arriaga, *Estudios o Caprichos*/ii/87–107. © Union Musical Española, n.d. Used by permission of the publisher.

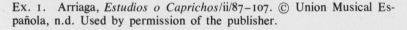

Two Spanish composers who, for the most part, lived outside of Spain but made a small contribution to nineteenth-century Spanish pianism were CARLOS ASENCIO (b. 1788) and MANUEL AGUILAR (1824–1904). Asencio, originally of Madrid, moved to Palermo, Sicily, where he published a *Scuola per ben suonare il piano forte*[3] in 1815. Aguilar was born of Spanish parents in Clapham, England. He studied harmony and composition in Frankfurt, Germany, and performed as a concert pianist in the Gewandhaus of Leipzig in 1848. He later returned to England, established a piano studio in London, and was known for his Beethoven concerts. Aguilar wrote sonatas and fantasies for the piano.[4]

PEDRO ALBÉNIZ (1795–1855), son of Mateo Albéniz, was the founder of the modern Spanish school of piano playing. He was born in Logroño and studied first with his father. Mateo Albéniz became choirmaster and organist of the church of Santa María in Guipúzcoa, where, at age ten, young Pedro was named organist of the parish of San Vicente. At thirteen he placed second as a contender for the post of organist at the basilica of Santiago in Bilbao.

P. Albéniz made notable progress in his study of composition and soon moved to Paris, where he studied with Henri Herz and Friedrich Kalkbrenner.[5] The night he arrived in Paris, he was presented to Rossini, who immediately tested him for his musical capabilities. Favorably impressed, Rossini took him under his protection and made him cembalist for his operas.

P. Albéniz returned to Spain in 1829 to become chapelmaster of the church of Santa María in San Sebastián. Early in 1830, he went to Madrid with the distinguished violinist Escudero to give several concerts, all of which were well received. Later in 1830 he was appointed *maestro de piano y acompañamiento* of the Conservatorio de Música de María Cristina. He had previously been consulted about the creation of this conservatory. In 1834, he became chief organist of the Royal Chapel.

In 1840, P. Albéniz's *Método de Piano* was adopted for the training of piano students at the conservatory.[6] It was praised by many distinguished artists, among them Sigismund Thalberg.[7] By 1841,

P. Albéniz had been named *maestro de piano* for Queen Isabel II and her sister María Luisa Fernanda.

P. Albéniz's major works for piano include *Rondó brillante á la Tirana*, Op. 25; *Rondó brillante sobre la canción del Trípili*, Op. 26; several fantasias on operatic themes, e.g., *Fantasía elegante sobre motivos de I Puritani*, Op. 29; and *Fantasía brillante sobre motivos de Lucia di Lammermoor*, Op. 34. In addition, he wrote several works for piano four hands, most of which are fantasias on operatic themes; and for piano with two violins, viola, and cello, again many of them fantasias on operatic themes.[8]

Being in Paris in the early nineteenth century, P. Albéniz was understandably caught up in the craze for writing piano fantasias on operatic themes.[9] His *Fantasía brillante sobre motivos de Lucia di Lammermoor* is typical of what audiences at that time wanted to hear. It is divided into the following major sections: Introduction, Funeral March from the final scene of Act III, hunting motive near the opening of Act I, and Edgardo's famous aria "Tu che a Dio spiegasti l'ali" from the conclusion of the opera. Ex. 2 shows a passage from the final section of the fantasia. Edgardo's beautiful melody is adorned with sweeping arpeggios in the left hand. It is noteworthy that Liszt based his *Reminiscences de Lucia di Lammermoor* entirely on the famous sextet from Act II, scene 2, while P. Albéniz completely by-passed this noted source of thematic material.

Though P. Albéniz's fantasias on operatic themes are not pathologically difficult, as some might contend Liszt's are,[10] they do tend to tax the ability of the performer at times. They feature many long passages of left-hand tremolos, difficult leaps, fast scalar passages, wide-ranging arpeggios, and awkward interval expansions in the left hand, in addition to containing passages that appear to have been merely transcribed from the orchestral version.

Ex. 2.   P. Albéniz, *Fantasía brillante sobre motivos de Lucia di Lammermoor*/129–134.

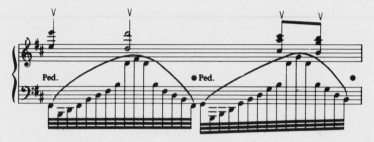

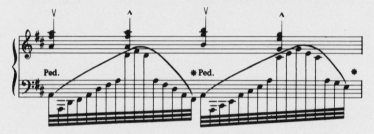

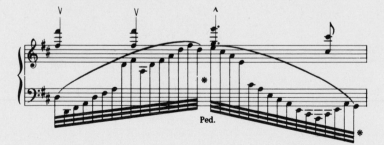

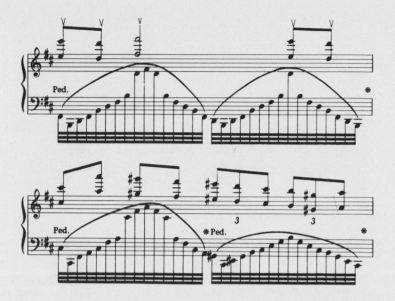

EUGENIO GÓMEZ (b. 1802), of Alcañices, near Zamora, moved to Seville in 1824, where he eventually became one of the organists of the cathedral and director of the theater. He supposedly had great facility at the keyboard and wrote sonatas and a number of other works of great difficulty for the piano. These works probably have remained unpublished.[11]

SANTIAGO DE MASARNAU (1805–1880), originally of Madrid, composed the music for a Mass at age eight. He later studied in Granada and again in Madrid. He then moved to London and Paris, where he became a part of the intellectual environs of the day. Before his return to Spain in 1829, Masarnáu became friends with Rossini, Bellini, Moscheles, and Chopin. For the piano, he composed sonatas, ballades, songs, *La Ricordanza, El canto de las driadas,* a nocturne entitled *Spleen* that supposedly impressed Mendelssohn,[12] and nine waltzes entitled *Le Parnasse,* representing the nine muses.[13]

FLORENCIO LAHOZ (1815–1868), of Alagón, Zaragoza, studied music first locally with his father, an organist, then later in

Madrid. Lahoz composed a symphony, masses, *zarzuelas,* and numerous works for piano.[14] The *Gaceta Musical de Madrid,* 1856, mentions several salon pieces by Lahoz, among them *Fantasía sobre motivos de Macbeth* and *Fantasía de Luisa Miller;* and the Biblioteca Nacional contains a copy of his *Gran Jota Aragonesa.*

JOSÉ MIRÓ (1815–1879), another of Spain's great salon pianists, was born in Cádiz.[15] Noting that the young José had a gift for music, his family entrusted his first music lessons to one Padre Vargas. Later, Miró studied with Eugenio Gómez, organist of the Cathedral of Seville. His progress in piano and counterpoint went so rapidly that, at age eighteen, he became Gómez's assistant director of the opera at the theater in Seville.

In 1829, Miró went to Paris, where he studied with Kalkbrenner and came into contact with other famous pianists, such as Hummel, Bertini, Herz, Chopin, and Döhler. Repeatedly, he was proclaimed by the press as one of the most outstanding pianists of the day. He gave recitals in France, Holland, Belgium, and England.

Miró returned to Spain in 1842. Joaquin Espin gives the following information regarding a concert given by Miró in Madrid, May 18, 1842:

> The pieces that he played on this delightful night were a *Fantasía sobre motivos del Guglielmo Tell;* a Nocturne by Döhler, which comprises a study for the left hand; another large study for both hands, the trill capricho; and a large fantasia by Thalberg on the *Plegaria del Moisés.* To enumerate the beauties that Miró performed on this night is, on all points, impossible in one article—the clarity and brilliance of his execution; the fierceness and energy that he showed in the loud passages; the delicateness in the *andantes* and *cantabiles;* the execution being so rapid and flowery in the agile passages; the prolonged trill in an amazing manner for more than one hundred measures, at the same time that the other fingers bring out an expressive, sustained melody; so marvelous those distinct passages blended with all the fire of genius in order to amaze the spectators, who, astonished and surprised on hearing such marvelous sounds, don't dare even to breathe so as not to miss a single note. What does all this prove to us? [It proves] that, concerning the piano, Miró has made the

Madrid public feel what it had not felt before this night; that
Miró is a celebrity, an artist of great merit, and that lucky is the
country that has sons who stir up their ancient artistic glories,
causing admiration wherever one might have the fortune of hearing him.[16]

After several concerts in Madrid, Miró was decorated by the queen
with the cross of the Order of Isabel the Catholic. Very prestigious
artists, including Pedro Albéniz, bestowed lavish praise upon him.

After traveling to the principal cities of Spain, he went to Lisbon,
where he gave four concerts in the theater of San Carlos. Continu-
ing his tour, he went to the United States and played in New York,
Philadelphia, and Boston. From there he went to Havana, Cuba, to
be named director of the music section of the Liceo in 1844. In
1854, Miró returned to Madrid, where he was appointed professor
of piano at the Royal Conservatory. In 1856, he published a piano
method that was adopted as the text for the classes of the conservatory.

Some of his most noted works for piano were *Fantasías grandes*
on themes from *Il Crociato in Egitto, Semiramide, Anna Bolena,*
and *Norma*.[17] Saldoni noted that Miró composed a large number of
works for piano but that many of them were never published.[18] The
Biblioteca Nacional in Madrid contains only Miró's piano method
and the *Cinco valses brillantes,* published in *La Iberia Musical,*
1842.

NICOLÁS LEDESMA (1791–1883), of Grisel, Tarragona, began
his musical studies, like so many Spanish composers, with the
music directors of the local church. Later, he went to Zaragoza to
study organ with Ramón Ferrañac. At age sixteen he became organist and choir director at the Colegiata de Borja and two years
later changed to an equal position in Tafalla. By 1830 he had been
appointed organist at the Cathedral of Bilbao.

Ledesma was a very celebrated church musician in his day, having written numerous sacred works, the most noted being his
Stabat Mater.[19] He also composed *12 estudios para piano,* which
were adopted for use at the Madrid Conservatory, but the bulk of
his piano music comes from a collection entitled *Repertorio or-*

gánico. The title may seem puzzling at first, but, as with many Spanish keyboard works of the time, the sonatas in the anthology are listed "para piano u órgano."

The large collection of keyboard music contains 24 sonatinas, six grand sonatas, and three *Juegos de versos para salmos.*[20] Typical of the six grand sonatas is No. 1 in C major, displaying a first movement in sonata–allegro form, a second movement in modified sonata–allegro form (no development), and a third movement of theme and variations. Occasional low bass notes are provided for the pedals of the organ, but generally the style is pianistic, complete with running broken octaves.

The first movement opens in symphonic style with bold octaves, a motive almost identical to the opening of Baguer's Sonata in G major. The second movement, possibly the strongest of the three, is in the parallel minor, C minor, and resembles some of Beethoven's slow movements, replete with ornate 64th notes (Ex. 3). The finale is in the key of the subdominant, F major, instead of the usual tonic. The variations, for the most part, are square-cut, but the final variation is unusual—a march superimposed on 3/4 meter.

Ledesma's sonatas border on what might be called *kitsch,* artistic material of low quality.[21] But they "are pleasing and unassuming, though at times they lack melodic inventiveness and sound structure. Completely un-Spanish, these sonatas are too often colored with the popular salon-music style of their day."[22] Still, they represent one little-known Spanish composer trying to keep the sonata tradition alive in nineteenth-century Spain.

PEDRO TINTORER (1814–1891), born in Palma de Mallorca, began his musical studies with Maestro Vilanova in Barcelona. In 1832, he entered the Madrid Conservatory, where he studied with Ramón Carnicer and Pedro Albéniz. In 1834 he studied with Pierre Zimmerman in Paris;[23] and in 1836 he set up residence in Lyon, France, where he studied with Franz Liszt for a year. In Lyon Tintorer supposedly taught piano sixteen hours a day.[24] Later, he returned to Barcelona to become professor of piano in the conservatory of the Liceo.

Ex. 3.   Ledesma, Sonata No. 1/ii/42–53.

Tintorer composed sacred music, symphonies, chamber music, and much salon music for piano, e.g., *Suspiros de un trovador, Conversación y vals,* and the grand salon waltz *Flor de España.*[25] He was also noted as a pedagogue, having written such didactic works as *Douze Grandes Études de Mécanisme et de Style, Curso Completo de Piano,* and *Gimnasia Diaria del Pianista.*[26]

Tintorer's *Flor de España* opens with a Spanish folk rhythm and *rasgueado* chords as if the work were going to be a dazzling nationalistic piece. But once past the opening chords and thunderous octaves, the air of Spain quickly disappears. Here we find a waltz in the "grand manner," with even a Rossini *crescendo* thrown in. Ex. 4 illustrates Tintorer's salon style, with effective right-hand figurations over a familiar descending bass pattern (mm. 120–137) and a syncopated right-hand melody (mm. 142–149), recalling Chopin's Waltz in A-Flat major, Op. 42.

MANUEL MARTÍ (1819–1873), of Vigo, in Galicia, was playing works by Kalkbrenner, Moscheles, and Herz by age fifteen. He had begun his studies with his uncle Antonio Martí, organist and choirmaster of the Colegiata of La Coruña, and later studied counterpoint with the noted Italian Mercadante.

In 1838, Martí made his debut as a pianist in Oporto, Portugal. Having been well received, he then toured other cities in Portugal. He lived in Lisbon for a while, becoming a professor of piano there, and in 1840 he received the "diploma de sócio de merito" from the Academia Filarmónica. In 1848, Martí went to Brazil, hired by the government to inspect the music programs in the province of Paraguay. In 1850, he returned to Europe.

Martí supposedly composed over 200 works by the year 1867,[27] but, as with José Miró, most of them were probably never published. The Biblioteca Nacional of Madrid contains only a series of six easy works from *Escuela recreativa de los pianistas* by Martí—miniature fantasies on operatic themes by Meyerbeer, Gounod, Flotow, and Verdi.

JUAN MARÍA GUELBENZU (1819–1886), of Pamplona, studied with his father, José Guelbenzu, an organist and teacher of harmony and composition. Later, Juan María moved to Paris to

Ex. 4. Tintorer, *Flor de España*/120–149.

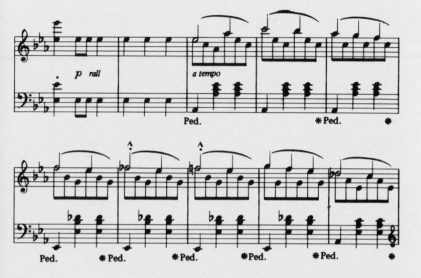

continue his studies with the pianist Émile Prudent. He achieved a favorable reputation as a pianist in Paris. In 1841 he returned to Spain and became the queen's pianist; in 1844 he was appointed organist of the Royal Chapel.

Guelbenzu is said to have contributed much to the musical culture of Spain. He was supposedly noted for his performances of the German classics, and he, along with Jesus de Monasterio, founded the Sociedad de Cuartetos de Música Clásica.[28] Guelbenzu composed a large number of sacred works for the service of the Royal Chapel as well as some works for piano. *Recuerdo vascongado* shows his reflections back to his native region.

JOSÉ ARANGUREN (1821–1903), of Bilbao, first studied solfège and piano under the direction of Nicolás Ledesma. In 1843, Aranguren went to Madrid, where he studied composition at the conservatory with Hilarión Eslava. In 1855, Aranguren issued his *Método de piano*, which went through several editions,[29] and in 1861, his *Prontuario para los cantantes é instrumentistas*, both of which were adopted by the Real Conservatorio. Also in 1861 he became a professor of harmony at the conservatory in Madrid.

Guía práctica de armonía was published in 1872 and *Nuevo método completo para piano* in 1894. In 1881, Aranguren returned to his native city of Bilbao, where he established a music publishing company.[30]

MARCIAL DEL ADALID (1826–1881), of La Coruña, Galicia, studied with Moscheles in London and with Chopin in Paris. One critic wrote that "his music shares in the London fogs and the brilliant sun of Spain."[31] Of this little-known Spanish composer, who wrote various works for piano, only a Sonatina for piano is preserved in the Biblioteca Nacional in Madrid.[32]

ADOLFO DE QUESADA (b. 1830), originally of Madrid, spent his early years in Cuba, where he studied piano with Miró. At age seven he gave his first recital. Later he returned to Europe, where he studied with Kalkbrenner, Thalberg, and Herz. He became a friend of Louis Moreau Gottschalk, the American pianist and visitor to Paris.[33] For the piano Quesada wrote *Valses artísticos; Escenas de la vida de una artista; Capricho romántico;* Sonata in E; *Allegro de concierto; Andante y rondó;* and *Grandes estudios de piano,* which was adopted as a text at the Madrid Conservatory. For two pianos, he wrote *Marcha,* dedicated to Wagner, and *Marcha poética,* dedicated to Liszt.[34]

DÁMASO ZABALZA (1830–1894), one of the most fashionable Spanish salon pianists of the nineteenth century, was born in Irurita, Navarra. He studied piano in Pamplona with Vidaola and later continued in Madrid, where he eventually taught piano at the Madrid Conservatory from 1857 until his death. Zabalza wrote numerous piano pieces, such as fantasias on themes from *Il Trovatore, Norma, Les Huguenots, Aida, Faust, La Traviata;* 24 Sonatinas; 12 Estudios; and numerous didactic works.[35]

FERMÍN MARÍA ALVAREZ (1833–1898), of Zaragoza, was a noted pianist and composer in Spanish aristocratic circles, in part because he married a lady of high society. For the piano, he wrote polkas, mazurkas, and salon waltzes, among them a *Domicile adoré* (Do Mi Si La Do Re).[36]

EDUARDO COMPTA (1835–1882), of Madrid, was a piano student of Pedro Albéniz at the Conservatorio de María Cristina. In 1856, he went to Paris, and in 1857 to Brussels, where he studied with Antoine Marmontel, Auguste Dupont, and François-Joseph Fétis. After giving a number of concerts in Holland, he returned to Paris in 1861, where he performed for Napoleon III and his court. In the same year, he went back to Spain to give many concerts on tour. In 1865, he was appointed professor at the Real Conservatorio in Madrid. According to Pedrell, he published several works for piano as well as a piano method.[37]

JUAN BAUTISTA PUJOL (1835–1898), a student of Pedro Tintorer, was born in Barcelona. In 1850, he went to the Paris Conservatory, where so many Spanish pianists of the century received their training. While in Paris, he won two prizes in piano competitions, and upon completing his studies there, he toured in France and Germany. In 1870, he returned to Barcelona and established a piano studio. Among his noted disciples were Isaac Albéniz and Granados.[38]

Pujol composed numerous salon pieces for piano, typical among them being his Fantasía–Mazurka *Rosas y Perlas*. He was especially known for his fantasias on themes from *L'Africaine* (Meyerbeer) and *Faust* (Gounod).[39] His *Grand Fantasia* on themes from *Faust,* dedicated to Eduardo Compta, gives evidence that Pujol indeed must have had tremendous facility at the keyboard. This popular ''crowd-pleaser'' contains roaring chromatic passages sandwiched between principal themes, fast-running octaves, treacherous right-hand embellishments, and long passages of similar figurations without relief for the performer.

Pujol organized his *Faust* fantasia into the following divisions: (1) themes from the Soldiers' Chorus, Act IV, scene 3, and the Chorale of the Swords, Act II; (2) music from the Love Duet, Act III; (3) Spinning Wheel music from Act I with the Love Duet theme of Act III, as stated in the Gounod score; (4) music of the fair, opening of Act II; (5) Soldiers' Chorus, Act IV, scene 3. Ex. 5 shows Pujol's difficult embellishments surrounding music from the Love Duet of Act III. While Liszt did use the Spinning Wheel

Ex. 5.   Pujol, *Faust*/72–76.

music from Act I in his *Walzer aus der Oper Faust von Gounod,* he concentrated mainly on the waltz material of Act II, a source of thematic material not used by Pujol in his fantasia.

While audiences were still calling for more fantasias on operatic motives, one writer in Spain was pleading for an end to this type of piano music. A certain M. D. de Quijano wrote an article entitled "¡No mas fantasías sobre motivos de operas!" ("No More Fantasies on Motives from Operas!") in the *Abeja Montañesa* of Santander.[40] The article begins:

> If any of the old players of the psaltery were to come to life before a grand piano of Erard, on which was being performed one of the *fantasías brillantes* that flood the salon concerts today, so great would be his astonishment that he would try to flee, wondering if it [grand piano] were a musical instrument, or if he were in the midst of a storm.
>
> The roars of the wind depicted by chromatic scales, the hurricane by arpeggios, and the thunder by chords of all types, would not allow his hearing, fatigued by the noise of the storm, to perceive the parts of a theme snatched perhaps from some sublime melodic inspiration and confused there in the midst of the whirlwind of an amazing performance that many times has no more artistic merit than that of a notable juggler.

Señor Quijano asks that pianists/composers make better use of their time, instead of borrowing another composer's inspiration just to add arpeggios, scales, etc. He even makes a satirical comparison to literature when he states, "What would be said if a *fantasía sobre motivos del D. Quijote* were published and all the merit of the work were reduced to combine some of the many sentences of the sublime work by the immortal Cervantes with a revelry of wordy insult?'' Nevertheless, piano fantasies on themes from operas continued to be written in Spain, as we shall see with Antonio Nicolau, a student of Pujol.

FELIPE PEDRELL (1841–1922), born in Tortosa, was one of Spain's most distinguished and learned musicians. He is mentioned here, not because of his contribution to Spanish piano music, but because of the tremendous influence he had on later Spanish composers. Pedrell became a professor of music history at the Madrid Conservatory, a post he held until 1894.

Pedrell believed, as did his eighteenth-century predecessor Eximeno, that every country should build its music on the foundation of native song. His lifelong dream was to create a great Spanish musical art of truly national character. For Pedrell, as for the Czech Janáček, the Hungarian Bartók, and the English Vaughan Williams, the exploration of the living folklore of the homeland was no end in itself. He considered it to be of the utmost importance for the inspiration of the Spanish "artist of the future," in his efforts to hasten the rebirth of his country's music.[41]

Pedrell composed a few works for piano—*Cuatro melodías características* (1862), *Estudios melódicos* (1866, 1867), *Esquisses symphoniques* (1867), mazurkas, nocturnes, waltzes—but he is chiefly remembered for his stage works, musical scholarship, and influence on such composers as Isaac Albéniz and Enrique Granados.[42]

TEOBALDO POWER (1848–1884), of Irish descent, was born in Santa Cruz, Tenerife, in the Canary Islands. At age seven he began musical studies with his father, and by age eleven he was already known as a pianist in Madrid and Barcelona. In 1862, the Diputación Provincial of Barcelona sent him to the Paris Conservatory, where he studied piano with Marmontel. Later, he returned to Spain to give concerts in Madrid, other provinces, and Portugal. Before his short life ended, Power became organist of the Royal

Chapel in Madrid and a professor of piano at the Madrid Conservatory.

Power's principal works for piano include *Cantos canarios, Gran Galop de Concierto, Scherzo de Concierto,* and *Grand Sonate* in four movements.[43] *Gran Galop de Concierto* is a period piece in the salon style, with facile patterns covering the entire range of the keyboard; but *Grand Sonate* in C minor is Power's real *tour de force,* a major Romantic work from Spain. Except for the sonatas of Ledesma and Isaac Albéniz, the Spanish sonata had all but disappeared in the latter part of the nineteenth century. Power's sonata has the following design: first movement—sonata–allegro form; second movement—ternary form; third movement—*Scherzino* (Scherzo and Trio); fourth movement—three-part sectional.

The first movement features a *perpetuum mobile* figure for the principal theme (Ex. 6), contrasted with a songful second theme placed in the tenor register of the piano. The second movement, *Andante,* tends to be a bit saccharine and thick in texture, though balanced in form. The third movement is marked *Scherzino,* a term used by I. Albéniz in his Sonata No. 4. Power's movement shows the typical elements of the scherzo and trio design, except that the trio section is four times as long as the scherzo section, thus the title. The scherzo features parallel first-inversion chords, while the trio part has an element of Spanish folk music. The finale, the weakest movement with respect to form, is composed of three different sections joined together, all technically difficult. The middle section proves to be the most difficult, with a relentless octave pattern divided between the two hands in order to bring out the theme (Ex. 7).

In view of the numerous studies listed in the *Catálogo de la Biblioteca Musical* of Madrid, ROBUSTIANO MONTALBÁN (1850–1937) must have been an important piano pedagogue in Spain during the late nineteenth and early twentieth centuries.[44] Unfortunately, little biographical information is available on this composer of Torrelaguna. However, the Biblioteca Nacional in

Ex. 6. Power, *Grand Sonate*/i/1–19.

Madrid preserves a salon piece by Montalbán entitled *Los cantares de mi patria, Fantasía sobre motivos españoles*. The work is divided into several sections, each characterizing specific regions of Spain. The introduction is based on the folk song "El Vito";[45] then follow five sections depicting typical melodies and rhythms from Aragon, Galicia, Madrid, Andalucía (based on "El Vito"), and again Aragon.

Ex. 7. Power, *Grand Sonate*/iv/32–45.

EMILIO SERRANO (1850–1939), born in Vitoria, studied in the Escuela Española de Bellas Artes in Rome and later became a professor of composition at the Madrid Conservatory.[46] He was also court pianist to the Infanta Isabel, Countess of Girgenti, and director of the Royal Opera in Madrid.[47] Though noted more for his work in the field of opera, he wrote several salon pieces for piano, which can be found at the Biblioteca Nacional and Biblioteca Musical in Madrid.

JOSÉ TRAGÓ (1857–1934), of Madrid, studied piano with Eduardo Compta and harmony with José Aranguren at the Madrid Conservatory. Afterwards, he went to the Paris Conservatory, where he became known as a concert pianist. He toured in other cities in France as well. Upon returning to Spain, he accompanied various artists, among them the eminent violinist Pablo Sarasate. Eventually Tragó became a professor of piano at the Madrid Conservatory, where he taught such notable students as Manuel de Falla and Joaquin Turina. Although Tragó composed works for the piano, he is mostly remembered as a pedagogue.[48]

ANTONIO NICOLAU (1858–1933), of Barcelona, began his musical studies with the noted pianist Juan Bautista Pujol. Later, he continued his studies in Paris, where he was known for his symphonic poems. In 1886 he returned to Barcelona. There he conducted many symphonic concerts and took charge of the Sociedad Catalana de Conciertos. In 1896 he was named director of the Escuela Municipal de Música, a post he held until his death.

Although Nicolau was noted more for his symphonic music, operas, and choral music, his piano fantasia on *Roberto il Diavolo* (Meyerbeer) should be mentioned.[49] Being dedicated to his teacher Juan B. Pujol, it follows in the tradition of the piano fantasia based on themes from operas. Though it is a flashy work, it is by no means as difficult as the *Faust* fantasia by Pujol. However, Nicolau's fantasia does have its moments of technical difficulty, especially the long passage of trills and *fioratura* writing. Ex. 8 illustrates Nicolau's idiomatic writing, featuring a sonorous melody in the bass dressed with effective chord patterns that sweep up and down the keyboard. Though not technically difficult, this passage is quite virtuosic and altogether pleasing.[50]

ANTONIO NOGUERA (1860–1904) was born in Palma, Ma-

Ex. 8.   Nicolau, *Roberto il Diavolo*/55–63.

llorca. He became a friend of Pedrell and was equally as enthusias-
tic about reviving the Spanish sacred polyphony of the sixteenth

century. Noguera had a profound interest in the folk music of Mallorca, as evidenced in his piano work *Trois danses sur des airs populaires de l'Isle de majorque*.[51] He also wrote sonatas and smaller works for piano.[52]

FRANCISCO ALIÓ (1862–1908), of Barcelona, studied piano with Carlos Vidiella and composition with Antonio Nicolau. Alió was very interested in the study of Spanish folk song and wrote many songs and piano pieces that show the "national idiom." According to John Trend, Alió was a forerunner of the Spanish national school, to be followed by I. Albéniz and Granados.[53] His *Barcarola* for piano is an easy salon piece with only a touch of the folk element, but more of the stereotype harmonies associated with this vintage. Other piano works include *Nota de color, Ballet, Ball del ciri*,[54] and *Marxa fantástica*.

FEDERICO OLMEDA (1865–1909), a native of Burgo de Osma, was a music historian, organist, and composer. He became organist at Tudela, Navarra, and Burgos, as well as *maestro de capilla* at the Convent of the Descalzas in Madrid. He, along with Pedrell, worked in the area of early polyphony and Spanish folk song.

Olmeda wrote the following works for piano: *Rimas* (32 pieces inspired by the poetry of Bécquer), *Scènes nocturnes, zortzicos*, waltzes, and *Sonate Espagnole*.[55] This last work deserves more attention because it is one of the few large works of its kind among a host of small salon pieces written by Spanish composers at the turn of the century.

Sonate Espagnole in A major contains three movements, all showing Spanish folk influence, as the title suggests. The first movement, marked *Andante–canción*, is cast in ternary form. Here Olmeda has provided the attractive folk idea (principal theme) with an accompaniment that is a diminution of the main theme (see Ex. 9). The second movement, *Scherzo–zortzico*, is a traditional scherzo and trio design, but based entirely on the alluring rhythm (5/8) of the Basque *zortzico*. The finale, the longest and most difficult movement, displays the rhythm of the Andalusian *petenera* and features a captivating cadenza.

Ex. 9.   Olmeda, *Sonate Espagnole*/i/4–9.

ENRIQUE MORERA (1865–1942) was born in Barcelona but spent his youth in Buenos Aires, Argentina. On returning to Barcelona, he studied piano with Carlos Vidiella and Isaac Albéniz and composition with Pedrell. Later he studied at the Brussels Conservatory. Though he is chiefly remembered for his larger works— operas, symphonies, and choral works—his piano arrangements of some of his noted *sardanas* give a colorful introduction to the national dance of Cataluña.[56]

JOAQUÍN LARREGLA (1865–1945), of Lumbier, Navarra, studied piano with Zabalza and harmony with Aranguren at the Madrid Conservatory. He gave numerous solo piano recitals in Spain and also accompanied Sarasate. He eventually became a professor of piano at the Madrid Conservatory.

Larregla wrote many works for piano, including *¡Viva Navarra!, Tarantela, Recuerdos de Italia, Album de Piezas Sinfónicas, Navarra montañesa,* and *Rapsodia asturiana.*[57] The celebrated jota *¡Viva Navarra!* was immediately popular when it first came out, and rightly so. It is one of the most delightful Spanish salon pieces available, having all the colorful rhythms and melodies that appeal to the general audience.[58] Ex. 10 shows such a passage,

which contains an appealing rhythmic figure accompanying a
"Spanish" melody that soars in the tenor register of the piano.

Ex. 10.   Larregla, *¡Viva Navarra!*/82–91. © 1954. Used by permission of
the publisher, Union Musical Española.

JACINTO MANZANARES (1872–1937), or Corera, Logroño,
studied with Zabalza at the Madrid Conservatory. Later, he toured
as a concert pianist and became director of the Escuela de Música
in Valladolid. He also taught composition at the Valencia Conservatory. Manzanares composed numerous works for piano, including *Andaluza, Nocturno, Pensamiento, Scherzo, Impromptu,
Oriental,* and a sonata.[59]

JOAQUÍN MALATS (1872–1912), of Barcelona, studied piano
with Juan B. Pujol at the Escuela Municipal de Música in his native
city. Later, he went on to the Paris Conservatory, where he won
prizes for his superb piano playing. He soon became known all
over Europe, and in 1905 he toured in America.

Malats wrote several works for piano, all light salon music, but
he was most noted for his interpretation of I. Albéniz's piano
music. He performed the complete *Iberia,* an amazing feat by any
standards, and thus stimulated public interest in the works of his
famous compatriot.

Isaac Albéniz

ISAAC ALBÉNIZ (1860–1909), one of Spain's greatest pianist/ composers, was born in Camprodón, Gerona. His musical talents were evident at such an early age that he resembled a Mozartean prodigy. He gave his first piano recital at age four and was composing by age seven. Naturally, his parents took advantage of his talents, and he was constantly exploited. It was not long before young Isaac began running away from home and going on his own concert tours. At first, it was only in Spain, but while in Cádiz, he stowed away on a ship and eventually found himself in Buenos Aires, Argentina.

In Argentina, at age twelve, Albéniz began an international concert tour that took him to Cuba, New York, and even as far away as San Francisco by 1874. In the same year, he made his way back to Europe, where he studied with Carl Reinecke in Leipzig. With some help from the Spanish government, he continued at the Brussels Conservatory, won first prize for piano playing there, and then went to study with Liszt in Weimar and Rome. By age twenty, he was touring as a mature virtuoso.

In 1885, he studied composition with Felipe Pedrell, who imparted to him the inherent values of Spanish folk music. By 1893, Albéniz had settled in Paris, where he became friends with Chausson, Fauré, Dukas, and d'Indy and eventually taught piano at the Schola Cantorum.

It is not known exactly how many works Albéniz composed for the piano, he being such a fluent composer, but it has been estimated that he published about 250.[60] It is unusual, however, that Albéniz composed most of them in the facile salon style, until the last three years of his life, when he completed the mammoth four books of *Iberia,* one of the greatest contributions to Spanish piano literature. Before discussing that most famous work, we should mention some of his earlier works.

Albéniz composed five sonatas for piano solo, but these works have been overshadowed by what Wilfred Mellers calls "postcard music" (trivial Spanish salon music).[61] William Newman tells us that they were probably written between 1883 and 1886 in Albéniz's shift to more serious composition.[62] Of Sonata No. 1, Op. 28, only the scherzo movement can be found today; of Sonata No. 2, nothing seems to be known; Sonatas Nos. 3, 4, and 5 are in three and four movements. Unlike many of Albéniz's salon pieces and *Iberia*, the sonatas contain no hint of the popular Spanish rhythms and melodic elements, but "their craftsmanship in harmony, scoring and voice-leading is beyond reproach."[63]

The *Suite Española* is one of Albéniz's best Hispanic collections. It features works that invoke the colorful rhythms of Granada, Cataluña, Seville, Cádiz, Asturias, Aragon, Castilla, and even Cuba. "Asturias" *(Leyenda)* and "Castilla" *(Seguidillas)* have proved to be the most successful works in this salon collection, which is representative of Albéniz's stylization of Spanish traditional idioms.

La Vega, part of an unfinished suite called *Alhambra,* was written in 1889 and shows Albéniz's transition to the gardens of the flatlands around Granada. The music suggests the counterpoint and chromaticism of Franck, with elements of the Andalusian *petenera.* Henri Collet reports that it has been compared with *Islamey,* the noted virtuoso piano work by the Russian Mily Balakirev.[64]

Azulejos ("Glazed Tiles") and *Navarra* were both incomplete when Albéniz died. The former, with its Moorish influences, was completed by Enrique Granados. The latter, completed by Déodat de Sévérac, reflects the rhythm of the *jota* from Navarra.[65]

Iberia, Albéniz's unquestionable masterpiece, subtitled "Twelve New Impressions," was published in four books from 1906 to 1909. All the pieces are of formidable technical difficulty and place demands on the best of artists. Collet, an ardent propagandist of the Spanish national school, relates that one day Manuel de Falla and Ricardo Viñes met Albéniz in the street in Paris, in a perfectly heartbroken state. He confided to them the cause of his sorrow, "Last night I came near burning the manuscripts of *Iberia,* for I saw that what I had written was unplayable."[66] Edgar Istel speaks of the technical difficulties in *Iberia* as "horrific" and says that only virtuosos of the very first rank are able to master them. Blanche Selva, one of the first interpreters of *Iberia,* repeatedly told Albéniz: "This cannot be played," to which Albéniz replied, "You shall play it."[67]

The twelve pieces of *Iberia* are picturesque descriptions of Spanish scenes and landscapes, mostly centered around Andalusia. They employ characteristic dance rhythms, many of which alternate with a lyrical vocal refrain, or *copla,* and often are combined contrapuntally with the *copla* toward the end of the movement. *Evocación,* the opening work of Book I, is the only work that does not refer by title to a place or regional style. It serves more as an introduction to the suite. However, it contrasts two distinct melodies that imply regional dance rhythms, the first a *fandanguillo* and the second a *jota navarra.*[68] *Evocación* has elements of the sonata principle within its guise of Impressionism (whole-tone passages, harmonic planing of augmented triads, and long pedal tones). Though technically easier than the other pieces in *Iberia,* *Evocación* is in the difficult key of A-flat minor.

El Puerto, named for El Puerto de Santa María, a fishing village near Cádiz, is in ternary form. Three dance rhythms make this work immediately appealing—the *polo* (mm. 11–17, 25–40), *bulerías* (mm. 17–24, 41–54), and *siguiriyas gitanas* (mm. 55–74). Albéniz makes effective use of whole-tone harmonies combined with the French augmented-sixth chord of D-flat for the retransition to the initial theme.

Corpus Christi en Sevilla (also titled *Fête-Dieu à Seville*), the last piece in Book I, opens with a marchlike theme, signifying the Corpus Christi procession winding its way through the narrow streets of Seville. Typical of the processions in this Andalusian city are the *saetas* (literally "arrows of song"), semi-improvised religious songs that punctuate the celebration. Thus, Albéniz interjects a piercing *saeta* in fortissimo octaves against a difficult pattern written on two staves above it (see Ex. 11).

Ex. 11.   Albéniz, *Corpus Christi en Sevilla*/83–94. Used by permission of Belwin Mills Publishing Corp.

Book II of *Iberia* opens with *Rondeña,* which bears the name of a dance from the Andalusian city of Ronda. The *rondeña,* a variant of the *fandango,* like so many Spanish dances, is characterized by the alternation of measures of 6/8 and 3/4. The essence of this movement is the vacillation between the attractive dance patterns and the lyrical *copla,* both of which are combined near the end.

Almería, relating to the Andalusian seaport, features the rhythm of the *tarantas,* a dance characteristic of the region of Almería, contrasted with a lyrical *copla.* Structurally, Albéniz uses a free adaptation of sonata form.

Triana, which also has elements of the sonata principle, is named for the gypsy quarter of Seville and has always been one of the most popular movements from *Iberia.* It features a *paso doble* in the opening followed later by and at times combined with a *marcha torera* (toreador march), according to Gilbert Chase.[69] In emulating the guitar, castanets, and tambourine, Albéniz has created an irresistible masterpiece in *Triana.*

El Albaicín, the first work of Book III, is named for the gypsy quarter in Granada. It contrasts the rhythms of the *bulerías* with a haunting *cante jondo* melody,[70] which moves within the characteristic narrow range of a sixth. Chase states that *El Albaicín* is the most beautiful and original of all the pieces in *Iberia,*[71] and Debussy was so struck by it that he wrote:

> Few works of music equal *El Albaicín* from the third volume of *Iberia,* where one recaptures the atmosphere of those evenings of Spain which exude the odors of flowers and brandy. . . . It is like the muffled sounds of a guitar sighing in the night, with abrupt awakenings, nervous starts. Without exactly using popular themes, this music comes from one who has drunk of them, heard them, up to the point of making them pass into his music so that it is impossible to perceive the line of demarcation.[72]

El Polo, the name of a melancholy Andalusian song–dance form, also shows elements of the sonata principle. The score is marked *allegro melancólico* at the beginning, and Albéniz uses the French terms *sanglot* and *sanglotant,* indicating a feeling of sobbing for this traditional Andalusian music. To this sorrowful type of folk song, Albéniz adds interesting harmonic color, what Paul Mast has called the Iberian augmented-sixth chord. It is a combination of the French and German augmented-sixth chords, creating a five-note chord. Sometimes a sixth note is added as a ninth above the bass.[73] Ex. 12 shows Albéniz's use of the Iberian augmented-sixth chord in F minor resolving to the dominant (mm. 248–250).[74]

Ex. 12. Albéniz, *El Polo*/244–253. Used by permission of Belwin Mills Publishing Corp.

Lavapiés was supposedly the work that almost caused Albéniz to destroy the manuscript because of its difficulties and his belief that it was unplayable. It gets its title from one of Madrid's popular quarters, named for a church where the foot-washing ritual was performed on Holy Thursday. Albéniz directs that "this piece should be played joyfully and with freedom" in order to depict the *chulos* (people of that district), who are loud in manners and dress. Again, Albéniz uses the sonata principle for organization of his colorful ideas, this time with the rhythm of the *habanera*. *Lavapiés* is one of Albéniz's most dissonant works.

The fourth book of *Iberia,* in the opinion of Collet, contains "the most beautiful jewels of the collection." *Málaga,* named for the Andalusian city on the Costa del Sol, has themes charged with the music of the *malagueña,* another of the forms related to the *fan-dango.* Here Albéniz again contrasts a rhythmic section with a graceful *copla* and then contrapuntally combines the two later in the piece.

Collet has deemed *Jerez,* the second piece of Book Four, the most beautiful of all the works in *Iberia. Jerez* takes its name from the famous wine-producing center Jerez de la Frontera, near Cádiz.

(The English word *sherry* comes from the name.) *Jerez,* constructed on the principle of sonata form, opens with the pattern of a *soleares,* another dance associated with the gypsies of Andalusia (see Ex. 13).

Ex. 13. Albéniz, *Jerez*/1–6. Used by permission of Belwin Mills Publishing Corp.

Eritaña, the concluding work of *Iberia,* refers to the name of the Venta Eritaña, a popular inn on the outskirts of Seville. To describe this famous tavern, Albéniz employs the bright rhythms of the *sevillanas,* related to the *seguidillas.* This work makes the seventh piece of Iberia to employ principles of sonata form, but no lyrical *copla* impedes the gaiety of this remarkably bold work. Debussy was so taken by this work that he wrote:

> *Eritaña* is the joy of morning, the happy discovery of a tavern where the wine is cool. An ever-changing crowd passes, their bursts of laughter accompanied by the jingling of the tambourines. Never has music achieved such diversified, such

colorful, impressions; one's eyes close as though dazzled by be-
holding such a wealth of imagery.[75]

Paul Mast, in his theoretical analysis of *Iberia,* has found Albéniz
to be essentially a nationalist of Romanticism, not of Impressionism, stating that Albéniz's use of modality; parallel motion;
secundal, quartal, and added-tone sonorities; and bichords have
their origins in Andalusian folk music and that his use of the
whole-tone scale is generally tied to functional tonality and not to
coloristic writing.[76]

Enrique Granados

ENRIQUE GRANADOS (1867–1916) was born in Lérida,
Cataluña. He showed early signs of musical talent, and, after the
family moved to Barcelona, he studied with the famous Spanish
pianist Juan B. Pujol. Later he continued private piano lessons with
Charles de Bériot, one of the main teachers at the Paris Conservatory.

In 1889 Granados settled in Barcelona, but continued to give recitals in other parts of Spain and in Paris. He taught piano and
turned out many distinguished pupils, though he supposedly did not
enjoy teaching.[77] In 1900, he founded the Sociedad de Conciertos
Clásicos and directed its performances.

Granados had none of the thirst for adventure that the young
Albéniz had; in fact, Granados disliked traveling, especially by
boat. However, he did consent to attend the first performance of
his opera *Goyescas* in New York, and that was the beginning of a
tragic end for one of Spain's most revered composers. The time
was 1916, the middle of World War I. On their journey back to
Spain, Granados and his wife died when the *Sussex* was torpedoed
by a German submarine and sank.

Granados had several things in common with Albéniz: both were
Catalan by birth, outstanding pianists, and students of Pedrell, and
both had studied in Paris. But here the resemblance fades.
Granados generally did not have Albéniz's preference for Andalu-

sian music; Granados leaned more toward the Chopinesque, with Hispanic overtones as a means to an end. In the words of Gilbert Chase, "What the Alhambra was to Albéniz, Madrid was to Granados."[78] Granados was intoxicated by the Madrid of the days of Goya, and the *majos, majas,* and *manolería*—the flamboyant populace of Madrid. His suite *Goyescas* for piano, later expanded into an opera of the same name, and *Tonadillas al estilo antinguo,* for voice and piano, were both inspired by the paintings and sketches of Goya.

Though Granados's great works display his *madrileñismo,* feeling for the spirit of Madrid at a colorful and romantic period of its history, many of his well-known smaller works show the influence of Andalusian music; e.g., Spanish Dances Nos. 2 *(Oriental),* 5 *(Andaluza),* 11 *(Zambra),* and 12 *(Arabesca).* However, Granados does not show the "realism" of an Albéniz or a later Falla. His music is always tempered, more restrained, aristocratic, and Romantic. More usual are Granados's numerous salon pieces, such as *Escenas románticas, Escenas poéticas,* and *Valses poéticos.*

Granados's works for piano can be grouped into three distinct periods: the nationalistic, the Romantic, and the "goyesca."[79] The nationalistic epoch is represented by such works as *Album de piezas sobre aires populares* and *Danzas españolas.* The Romantic period features numerous salon pieces, e.g., *Allegro de Concierto, Escenas románticas,* and *Cuentos para la juventud.* The "goyesca" period contains the *Goyescas* for piano and the *Tonadillas* for voice.

Unlike Albéniz, Granados wrote no sonatas. However, he did write a composition of some dimension in his *Allegro de Concierto,* a work that reveals his great gift for improvisation, which he supposedly could keep up for hours.[80] Constructed on the principles of sonata form, this rhapsodic piece features arabesques, wide leaps, and other difficult patterns recalling the works of Liszt (see Ex. 14).

As with Albéniz, Granados's masterpiece for piano came near the end of his life. The suite *Goyescas* consists of six pieces pub-

Ex. 14. Granados, *Allegro de Concierto*/120–121. © 1930. Used by permission of the publisher, Union Musical Española.

lished in two volumes (1912–1914). In a letter to the Spanish pianist Joaquin Malats, Granados wrote:

> I have composed a collection of *Goyescas* of great sweep and difficulty. They are the reward of my efforts to arrive. They say I have arrived. I fell in love with Goya's psychology, with his palette. With him and with the Duchess of Alba; with his lady *maja,* with his models, with his quarrels, his loves, and his flirtations. The white rose of the cheeks, contrasted with the flaxen hair against the black velvet with buttons and loops; those bending bodies of the dancing creatures, hands of mother-of-pearl and of jasmine resting on jet trinkets, they have disturbed me. . . . [81]

Subtitled *Los Majos Enamorados* ("The Majos in Love"), *Goyescas* consists of two parts: I. *Los Requiebros* ("Flirtations"), *Coloquio en la Reja* ("Conversation at the Window"), *El Fandango de Candil* ("Fandango by Lamplight"), and *Quejas ó la Maja y el Ruiseñor* ("Complaints or the Maid and the Nightingale"); II. *El Amor y la Muerte* ("Love and Death") and *Serenata del Espectro*

("The Specter's Serenade"). The last two works Granados labeled "ballad" and "epilogue," respectively. A seventh piece, *El Pelele* ("The Dummy"), is also associated with the suite and available in piano arrangement. *El Pelele,* based on the music of the opening scene of the opera *Goyescas,* depicts the "man of straw" being tossed in the air by the *majas.*[82]

Los Requiebros, the opening work from *Goyescas,* contains two main themes, both taken from the *Tirana del Trípili* by Blas de Laserna (see Ex. 15).[83] Granados takes his thematic material from the passages "Con el tripili" and "Anda, chiquilla" in the Laserna song. Exx. 16 and 17 show Granados's brilliant pianistic use of this simple vocal material.[84]

Ex. 15.　Laserna, *Tirana del Trípili.*

In *Coloquio en la Reja,* a love duet, Granados instructs that the bass notes should imitate the guitar. Midway through he includes

EX. 16.   Granados, *Los Requiebros*/292–303. © 1972. Used by permission of the publisher, Union Musical Española.

EX. 17.   Granados, *Los Requiebros*/57–64. © 1972. Used by permission of the publisher, Union Musical Española.

an expressive *copla*. Toward the end of this movement, he recalls a triplet accompaniment from the preceding movement, which he marks in the score. Harmonically, *Coloquio en la Reja* is one of the

Ex. 18.   Granados, *Quejas ó la Maja y el Ruiseñor*/20–24. © 1972. Used
by permission of the publisher, Union Musical Española.

most colorful movements because of Granados's exquisite use of
augmented-sixth chords.

El Fandango de Candil, the most Andalusian movement of the
suite, is a stately *fandango* in ternary form with driving rhythms.
The brief middle section is broad and expansive in contrast to the
rhythmic opening section. The return to the initial idea includes a
highly ornate version of the *fandango*.

The conclusion of Part I, *Quejas ó la Maja y el Ruiseñor,* is
probably the best-known movement from *Goyescas* and, in the
words of Gilbert Chase, "one of Granados' most personal and most
poetic utterances."[85] Pedro Morales declared that "rarely has the
Spanish soul manifested itself so clearly in cultured music as in the
initial theme of *La Maja y el Ruiseñor.*"[86] This movement depicts a
dialogue between a maid *(maja)* and a nightingale, the latter represented by a cadenza at the end of the piece. Ex. 18 shows the song
of the *maja,* one of the most beautiful passages in all of Spanish
literature. It is also interesting to note that for this thoroughly
Romantic work, Granados chose the key of F-sharp minor, a fa-

vorite key for many Romantic composers who wrote works opening with an impassioned flow.[87]

The ballad *El Amor y la Muerte*, the first piece of Part II, consists primarily of themes from the other four movements, many of the interrelated themes marked by Granados in the score. Probably the most striking use of interrelated themes occurs in the nocturne-like *adagio* section in B-flat minor, where Granados employs a tragic transformation of the lovely *maja* melody over a simple syncopated accompaniment.

The concluding epilogue, *Serenata del Espectro*, also recalls themes from previous movements, the different setting of the *copla* from *Coloquio en la Reja* being the most exquisite. This movement being a sort of dance of death, Granados has subtly employed a fragment from the *Dies Irae* in the tenor register of the piano.[88] Since this is a *Spanish* dance of death, Granados has the phantom disappear with the sounding of the open strings of the guitar.

While Albéniz's *Iberia* is a series of separate pieces that can be played in any order, Granados's *Goyescas* is a cyclical suite, bound together by poetic and thematic unity. Granados's superb masterpiece requires a highly developed keyboard facility, very much akin to the brilliant, ornate side of the technique needed for Chopin's music. Ernest Newman also remarks that the basis of the technique is Chopin, but that the style has a polyphonic quality too often lacking in Chopin. One could not say of this music, as Wagner said of Chopin's, that it is "music for the right hand."[89] Ernest Newman remarks further, "but above all, the music is a gorgeous treat for the fingers, as all music that is the perfection of writing for its particular instrument is. It is difficult, but so beautifully laid out that it is always playable: one has the voluptuous sense of passing the fingers through masses of richly colored jewels. It is pianoforte music of the purest kind."[90]

Both Albéniz and Granados wrote smaller, salon-type works for piano in their earlier years and created monumental, virtuosic works toward the end of their short lives. With *Iberia* and *Goyescas*, they became the peers of such notable Romanticists as Chopin, Schumann, and Liszt.

Summary

During the first half of the nineteenth century, a few Spanish composers (e.g., C. Baguer, M. Ferrer, F.M. López, J. Prieto) continued to write light sonatas, but gradually the trend turned toward writing salon pieces and fantasies based on operatic themes. Just as audiences demanded these superficial works of Liszt, they expected them from Pedro Albéniz, the founder of the modern Spanish school of piano playing. It should be noted that this period marks the beginning of the Spanish pilgrimages to Paris for musical training. Unfortunately, during most of the nineteenth century, Spain cannot claim a Chopin, a Schumann, or a Brahms.

Following the paths set by Pedro Albéniz came other technically gifted pianist/composers such as José Miró, Juan Bautista Pujol, and Antonio Nicolau, who concludes a line of composers who wrote fantasies on operatic themes well into the twentieth century.

The descriptive character pieces of the masters eventually gave way to the saccharine salon pieces by many European composers, and in this regard the composers of Spain were no exception. Nineteenth-century Spanish piano music suffered, in general, at the hands of Italian opera, which had been well entrenched in Spain since Farinelli's arrival in 1737. Pedro Tintorer and Joaquín Larregla were noted for their virtuosic salon works. Had he lived longer, Juan Crisóstomo de Arriaga might have contributed more worthy pieces to nineteenth-century Spanish piano music.

After the eighteenth century, the sonata tradition in Spain might virtually have died had it not been for the meager attempts of Nicolás Ledesma *(Six Grande Sonates),* Teobaldo Power *(Grand Sonate* in C minor), and Federico Olmeda *(Sonate Espagnole).* Although Isaac Albéniz composed five sonatas, they are early works and do not reflect the true creative talents to be seen later in his nationalistic works. None of these works comes close to the skillful and imaginative use of material found in the sonatas of Chopin, Schumann, Liszt, or Brahms.

Three Spanish composers who continued the sonata tradition in the early twentieth century include Vicente Arregui (Sonata in F minor), Juli Garreta (Sonata in C minor), and Joaquín Turina, whose descriptive sonata, *Sanlúcar de Barrameda,* is an excellent work. As we move further into the twentieth century, more sonatas appear in the catalogue of works by Spanish composers, many of which represent some of the best in this genre since the eighteenth century, e.g., sonatas or sonatinas by Rodolfo Halffter, Joaquin Nin-Culmell, Jesús García Leoz, and Cristóbal Halffter.

During the latter part of the nineteenth century and the early years of the twentieth, Spain experienced a keyboard renaissance, its golden age of piano music. This rebirth came first with Albéniz and Granados and continued with Falla, Turina, and Mompou.

After the age of Soler and Blasco de Nebra, Spain had to wait over a hundred years for keyboard composers who could be called the peers of other European notables. With Albéniz and Granados came Spain's answer to Liszt and Chopin, respectively. Albéniz's *Iberia* stands as one of the most impressive and technically difficult works in all piano literature, and Granados's *Goyescas,* a work that reflects Spanish Romantic piano music at its height, also requires technical wizardry on the part of the performer.

CHAPTER THREE

Falla, Turina, Mompou, and Their Contemporaries

Manuel de Falla

MANUEL DE FALLA (1876–1946) was born in Cádiz. His father was a businessman from a family of bankers and shippers; and his mother, an excellent pianist, was Falla's first teacher. The young Falla was a gifted piano student. At age fourteen he gave his first concert, which included works of his own and the first Cádiz performance of Schumann's Piano Quartet, Op. 47. Later he moved to Madrid, where he studied with the noted teacher José Tragó.

Falla eventually came into contact with Felipe Pedrell, the new leader of Spanish nationalism. Falla wrote that he had been "full of joy to meet, finally, something in Spain that I had imagined finding since beginning my studies. I went to Pedrell to ask him to be my teacher, and to his teaching I owe the clearest, and firmest orientation of my work."[1]

On July 5, 1904 the Academia de las Bellas Artes of Madrid announced a prize for a one-act Spanish opera, the first contest of its kind. Shortly after, the piano dealers Casa Ortiz y Gussó announced through the Madrid Conservatory that a concert grand would be given as a prize for the best performance of a formidable list of works, including the usual Bach fugue, Beethoven sonata, and works by Schumann, Chopin, and others. The opera was to be submitted before sunset of March 31 the following spring, and the piano contest was to begin the next day. Falla needed to win both and did. The opera submitted was *La vida breve*. In the piano contest he was pitted against the best pianists in Spain, including Frank Marshall, pupil of Granados and later director of the Academia Granados. Falla's performance so moved the jury that he was awarded the prize on the spot by acclamation and without discussion.[2]

Falla, like so many other Spaniards, made the pilgrimage to Paris. There he was warmly received by Paul Dukas, who introduced him to Albéniz, an already famous figure in Paris. Later he met Fauré, Debussy, and Ravel. The support of these noted musicians was to be invaluable in many situations, e.g., when Falla received a note from the publishing house of Durand, "The messieurs Debussy, Ravel, and Dukas have spoken to me of your *Four Pieces for Piano*. If you would care to send them to us we will be happy to publish them." Durand offered him 300 francs for the works. "They paid you fifty francs more than they gave me for my quartet," said Debussy. "That's what they gave me for *The Sorcerer's Apprentice*," said Dukas. "They didn't pay me anything for my score of *Catalonia*," said Albéniz. "And they didn't want my quartet even as a gift," added Ravel. Durand published *Cuatro piezas españolas* in 1909.[3]

With the coming of World War I in 1914, Falla returned to Madrid, where he completed such important works as *El amor brujo*, *El sombrero de tres picos*, and *Noches en los jardines de españa*, a work begun before he went to Paris. During these years in Madrid, Falla enjoyed an ever-increasing reputation as a composer.

In 1922, he moved to Granada for more peace and tranquility. For his place of refuge, he chose the hill of the Alhambra. Falla left Granada only when obligations as a composer or soloist demanded it, e.g., the trips to Mallorca in 1933 and 1934 to participate in the Chopin festivals. In the summer of 1939 he moved to Argentina and lived there until his death in 1946.

Falla wrote only seven works for solo piano: *Serenata andaluza,* *Vals capricho, Nocturno, Allegro de concierto,*[4] *Cuatro piezas españolas, Fantasía bética,* and *Homenaje a Dukas.*[5] They are seldom played, but one frequently hears transcriptions for piano of the popular dances from *La vida breve, El amor brujo,* and *El sombrero de tres picos,* "The Ritual Fire Dance" being the best-known transcription.

Among the original works for solo piano, *Vals Capricho* is a weak, un-Spanish salon piece; but *Serenata andaluza,* a more colorful work, holds more interest. It opens with an evocative dotted figure that sets the stage for the ensuing lyrical Andalusian melody, which hints at Falla's later piece "Andaluza" from *Cuatro piezas españolas.*

Cuatro piezas españolas, published in 1909, had already been performed in 1908 at the Société Nationale by Ricardo Viñes, a Spanish virtuoso pianist and a champion of new music. Falla himself played them in 1911 at his first concert appearance in London.[6] They are dedicated to Albéniz, who died in the year of their publication, and bear a slight resemblance to the piano works of Falla's older colleague. "The similarities are analogous to those that would be found in paintings of the same landscape by two different artists. The objects represented would be identical, but the point of view, the personal vision, the colouring, the drawing, the emphasis, would make each painting a separate and distinct work of art."[7] Albéniz generally gave the pieces in *Iberia* the names of particular cities or districts within a city; Falla uses names relating to entire provinces ("Aragonesa," "Cubana," "Montañesa," and "Andaluza"), as Albéniz had done much earlier in his *Suite española.*

The first three works of *Cuatro piezas españolas* are in ternary form, while the fourth is more extended. For the opening piece, "Aragonesa," Falla employs the popular dance rhythm of the *jota* of Aragon. Its incessant triplet figure is unmistakable, and scarcely a measure is to be found without it.

The second piece, "Cubana," may seem out of place with the others, but one must remember that many reciprocal influences existed between Andalusia and the Antilles at one point in Spanish history. At times, it was often difficult to separate what belonged to the New World and what to the Old. Thus, Falla has given this work the rhythm of the *guajira,* the most typical Cuban dance, characterized by alternations of 6/8 and 3/4. He sometimes contrasts these meters simultaneously between the two hands, making this small character piece metrically complex.

The third piece, "Montañesa," evokes a landscape of the region of La Montaña near Santander. An exquisite Impressionistic introduction is followed by a lyrical section in the style of a Montañés folk song. Falla contrasts this tranquility with a fast dance section based on the folk melody "Baile a lo llano." After the return to the opening mood, he gives a brief hint ("as an echo") of the dance section at the close of the movement.

The final piece, "Andaluza," provides a striking contrast to the preceding one. It is marked *tres rhythmé et avec un sentiment sauvage* ("very rhythmic and with a savage feeling"). This feeling is inevitable from Falla's expert use of grace notes to give the opening chords a metallic "clang," suggesting the rasp of the guitar.

Julio Esteban contends that "Andaluza" is the most perfected of the four pieces because of its motivic development. Falla develops a familiar motive associated with Spanish folk music, an introductory call of the tonic chord repeated four times, with sharp accentuations on the first beat (see Ex. 1). He converts this motive into the main theme, employing different devices in its development (compare Ex. 1 with Exx. 2 and 3).[8] The contrasting secondary theme is a lyrical, florid evocation of *cante jondo* with an oscillating accompaniment figure. Falla bases this material on the Gypsy-Andalusian scale with its Phrygian characteristics (see Ex. 4). Structurally, "Andaluza" resembles sonata–allegro form, with contrasting themes and development, but the return to the opening material is in reverse order.

Ex. 1

Ex. 2. Falla, "Andaluza"/1–4. © 1909 Durand et Cie. Used by permission of Elkan-Vogel Co., Inc.

Ex. 3. Falla, "Andaluza"/79–85. © 1909 Durand et Cie. Used by permission of Elkan-Vogel Co., Inc.

Ex. 4.

Fantasía bética (1919), Falla's largest and most difficult composition for solo piano, is his last work in the Andalusian idiom and a synthesis of all he had written before in this style. *Provincia Baetica* was the ancient Roman name for Andalusia, thus the composition is an Andalusian fantasy. Gilbert Chase remarks that it has never been popular because professional pianists are afraid it may not prove effective enough and amateurs are afraid of its technical difficulties.[9]

From a structural standpoint, *Fantasía bética* proves not complex at all, being in ternary form, but the numerous arabesques, downward arpeggios, and glissandos make it a formidable work (see Ex. 5). In this work, Falla goes beyond the biting dissonances of "Andaluza" to a harsher, more percussive guitarlike strumming, much more severe than in most works by his Spanish contemporaries. It smacks of the primitive and is more akin at times to Bartók and Stravinsky.

Ex. 5.   Falla, *Fantasía bética*/17–22. © 1922 Chester Music. Used by permission.

Falla's last work for solo piano, *Homenaje a Dukas* (1935), bears no outward visible sign of Spanish origin, but continues the dissonant vein of *Fantasía bética* and resembles the style of the Harpsichord Concerto. It is marked to be played *in tempo severo,* and makes effective melodic use of grace notes.

Joaquín Turina

JOAQUÍN TURINA (1882–1949) was a native of Seville, located in the southern province of Andalusia. During his adolescent years, he studied piano with Enrique Rodríguez and harmony with Evaristo García Torres, choirmaster of the cathedral. These early years were preoccupied with the opera and operatic productions in the theater of San Fernando. On May 14, 1897, Turina participated in a concert in the Sociedad de Cuartetos. Between a quartet by Spohr and the *Escenas andaluzas* by Breton, the young lad from Seville obtained sensational success with his fantasy on *Moïses* by Thalberg. He was acclaimed by the local newspapers and acquired a local fame for pianistic virtuosity.[10]

From 1902 to 1905, Turina traveled back and forth from Seville to Madrid. It was during those years that he became friends with another Andalusian youth, Manuel de Falla. Turina began piano studies at the Madrid Conservatory with José Tragó, who was already Falla's teacher. Turina's Madrid years had one goal—Paris.

Turina arrived there to study at the Schola Cantorum in the autumn of 1905. On the advice of Joaquín Nin, he began piano work with Moritz Moszkowsky, who specialized in the understanding of Spanish music from a standard of salon virtuosity. At the time that Turina came to Paris, the musical environment was, to say the least, stimulating. Debussy had recently composed *La Mer,* and d'Indy had published an article on *Pélleas.* Although Debussy was not interested in getting involved with factions, the struggle between the Impressionists and the Schola Cantorum gave nourishment to sharp and picturesque incidents.[11]

The Schola Cantorum, under the direction of d'Indy, was born toward the end of the previous century with the aim of improving French church music and sustaining the traditions of Franck. Its rival, the Paris Conservatory, was directed at that time by Fauré and housed many of the followers of Debussy. While Turina and Falla maintained their friendship of the Madrid days, they differed musically. Falla had entered the Debussy orbit at the conservatory, but Turina was able to keep a balance between the traditions of Franck and the innovations of Debussy.

In October 1907 Turina participated in a significant concert with a string quartet founded by Armand Parent. The program included the Schumann Piano Quintet; Book I of Albéniz's *Iberia; Prelude, Chorale and Fugue* by Franck; and, in its first performance, Turina's Piano Quintet in G minor, his first edited work. Both Albéniz and Falla attended the performance. Turina reports their first meeting in an article contributed to *Vanguardia* of Barcelona in 1917. He describes Albéniz as a fat man with a long black beard, wearing a huge broad-brimmed sombrero, who swept Falla and himself away to a café on the rue Royale. At that moment, the greatest metamorphosis in Turina's life took place: "There I realized that music should be an art and not a diversion for the frivolity of women and the dissipation of men. We were three Spaniards gathered together in that corner of Paris, and it was our duty to fight bravely for the national music of our country."[12] This meeting resulted in a triple pact to write "musica española con vistas a Europa" ("Spanish music with vistas toward Europe").

In early March 1913 d'Indy delivered to Turina a certificate from the Schola Cantorum. Only a few days later, the Orquesta Sinfónica of Madrid, directed by Arbós, introduced Turina's *La procesión del rocío*. The work had to be repeated on the same program, and Arbós took it in triumph all through Spain. In 1915 another symphonic poem, *Evangelio de Navidad,* was performed in Madrid by the Orquesta Sinfónica. It is a more intimate work, reflecting a quieter Andalusian mood. The *Danzas fantásticas* (1920) have become popular, both in piano transcription and in their original form for orchestra; and Turina's *Sinfonía sevillana,* one of the many tributes to his place of birth, was awarded a prize in a competition at San Sebastián in 1920.

In addition to composing music, Turina wrote two important books that filled a vacuum at that time in Spain. *Enciclopedia musical abreviada* (1917), with a prologue by Manuel de Falla, has served many Spanish musicians in the study of music history and composition. The work is dedicated to d'Indy and is a summary of the teachings and experiences acquired at the Schola Cantorum. Later, Turina wrote *Tratado de composición* (1947), a more personal view, in the opinion of his biographer, Federico Sopeña.

When the Spanish Civil War broke out in 1936, Turina and his family spent many anxious days in Madrid. He and his chamber music colleagues used to meet in the home of Isabel and John Milanes, the British Vice-Consul in Madrid. The Milaneses kept open house for Spanish musicians during the revolution. Several of Turina's works received their first performances in their home, and one of them, *El cortijo*, was dedicated to the couple in a tribute to Anglo-Spanish friendship.[13] When the Comisaría general de la Música in the Ministerio de Educación Nacional was created in 1941, Turina was named its head.

Piano works constitute a significant part of Turina's total output: four sonatas, four fantasies, five sets of dances, five miscellaneous abstract works, and 38 descriptive works (five in one movement, 33 in the form of suites), a total of 55 published works for piano.[14]

Two of the piano sonatas have programmatic elements — *Sanlúcar de Barrameda (sonata pintoresca)*, Op. 24, and *Rincón mágico (desfile en forma de sonata)*, Op. 97, each in four movements. William S. Newman does not mention these sonatas in *The Sonata since Beethoven*, probably because the subtitles are lacking in certain listings of Turina's works. In any event, the omission is unfortunate, especially regarding *Sanlúcar de Barrameda*. Federico Sopeña states that this large sonata is "perhaps the most virtuosic work for piano in the Spanish repertoire, after the works of Albéniz."[15] Albert Lockwood also refers to *Sanlúcar de Barrameda* as a formidable concert sonata.[16]

The early *Sonata romántica (sobre un tema español)*, Op. 3, is in three movements. Turina characterized this sonata as "Romantic" "because he desired to combine in it the harmonic–vertical tendency of the Debussy school, the counterpoint and form of d'Indy, and the sentiment of the Spanish race."[17] He chose for his *tema español* the Spanish folk song "El Vito," which can be found in the second volume of *Vingt chants populaires* by Joaquín Nin. Winton Dean considers the first movement of this sonata, a theme and variations, as one of the most interesting of Turina's piano works.[18] *Sonata fantasía,* Op. 59, has only two movements and is dedicated to the Spanish musicologist José Subirá.

The four fantasies are all relatively late works. *Fantasía italiana,* Op. 75, and *Fantasía del reloj,* Op. 94,[19] are essentially descriptive suites. *Fantasía cinematográfica,* Op. 103, bears the subtitle *en forma de rondó,* and for the rondo theme, Turina employs one of his favorite dance rhythms, that of the Basque *zortzico.*[20] Turina dedicated his *Fantasía sobre cinco notas,* Op. 83, to Enrique Arbós on the occasion of the famed conductor's seventieth birthday.[21] It is based on the letters A–R–B–O–S, which equal the pitches A–D–B-flat–C–G. This work, later orchestrated, is the only abstract fantasy in the group.

As one might expect, Turina's dances are some of his most characteristically Hispanic contributions to the literature. This fact is immediately apparent from the title of the earliest set, *Tres danzas andaluzas,* Op. 8. Turina pays homage to another Spanish province in *Dos danzas sobre temas populares españolas,* Op. 41, one of which is based on the Basque national song, "El Árbol de Guernica." The two sets of Gypsy Dances, Op. 55 and Op. 84, are dedicated to José Cúbiles, a noted interpreter of Turina's piano music. Although these dances are basically descriptive movements evoking gypsy rituals, Turina employs authentic dance rhythms in certain movements, e.g., the *polo* in "Generalife" of Op. 55.[22] He reverted to the previous century for his *Bailete,* Op. 79, a cyclic suite of nineteenth-century dances. One dance of this set is a *bolero,* a dance rhythm made popular five years earlier by the Frenchman Ravel.

Most of Turina's abstract works for piano are a part of *Ciclo pianístico,* a large cycle that includes *Tocata y fuga,* Op. 50; *Partita en Do,* Op. 57; *Pieza romántica,* Op. 64; *Rapsodia sinfónica,* Op. 66, for piano and string orchestra; and *Preludios,* Op. 80. As the titles show, Turina drew some of his inspiration from Baroque instrumental forms, but he did include one descriptive work in the cycle, *El castillo de Almodóvar,* Op. 65, which was later orchestrated.

The largest category within the piano music is that of the descriptive works, mostly in the form of suites. One only has to read the titles of many of Turina's compositions—*Album de viaje,* Op. 15; *Mujeres españolas,* Op. 17; *Niñerías,* Op. 21, to name only a few—to see that he has given the words *album* and *suite* more significance than have many of his colleagues. Like Schumann, he made a special contribution to the literature for children.

The descriptive suites usually contain from five to eight movements. The programs are mostly geographical, often localized in Seville. There are three sets of female portraits; several series of childhood evocations; legends; and visits to the shoemaker, the circus,[23] and the radio station.

The preceding discussion should not lead one to believe that all Turina's descriptive works are small in scale. On the contrary, *Sevilla,* Op. 2; *El barrio de Santa Cruz,* Op. 33; and *Por las calles de Sevilla,* Op. 96, are large, technically difficult works. All three compositions evoke some aspect of Turina's native Seville, unique among them being *El Barrio de Santa Cruz.* This unusual work is a set of rhythmic variations on a multiple theme from whose motives Turina draws a set of pictorial impressions. Winton Dean goes so far as to single it out as one of Turina's best descriptive compositions.[24]

Turina obviously had a predilection for the descriptive. On the whole, he preferred to express himself musically through intimate, personal evocations, instead of through larger forms. As Walter Starkie points out, Turina did not look upon the piano as an instrument for great effects, but rather as a dear friend of long standing to whom he could pour out his confidences.[25] According to a music critic for the *Musical Times,* Turina's *Niñerías,* Op. 56, was written for the composer's children and "to be played to them, probably, rather than by them. They are not very difficult, but they need good technique and musicianship if they are to sound as simple as they should."[26] With further bearing on the smaller suites, a reviewer in the *Monthly Musical Record* writes that Turina's *Jardín de niños,* Op. 63, is no more for a child to play than is Schumann's *Kinderscenen.*[27]

The factors that most influenced the shaping of Turina's style are (1) the Andalusian idiom, or some other Spanish regional influence; (2) the post-Franckian atmosphere of the Schola Cantorum; and (3) the innovations of Debussy. At least one of these factors is likely to be present in his piano music, whether in the melody, harmony, rhythm, texture, or form. The Spanish flavor and nationalistic air of Turina's music, which derives chiefly from the Andalusian idiom, impresses itself on the listener immediately. Turina devoted himself entirely to writing nationalistic music after his memorable meeting with Albéniz and Falla in Paris in 1907.

He was first and foremost a composer of lyrical melodies. This observation is not surprising in light of his allegiance to nationalism, which was characterized to a large extent by exquisite Hispanic melodies. They often possess what the Spaniards call *evocación,* that is, "a sense of poetry or suggestiveness, something which can be felt rather than explained."[28]

The idea of *evocación* is indeed subjective, and for this writer, one of Turina's finest melodies that possesses this quality is in "Petenera," from *Tres danzas andaluzas,* Op. 8 (see Ex. 6). This thoroughly Hispanic melody, placed in the tenor register of the piano, is replete with syncopations of the hemiola type. It shows the characteristic Andalusian pattern of a descending minor tetrachord (la–sol–fa–mi) and has a predominance of conjunct motion. Melodies that evoke a particular mood or spirit also permeate the piano literature of Albéniz, Granados, and Falla.

Turina not only writes melodies that *sound* Spanish but also employs actual Spanish folk songs in his piano music, as in his *Sonata romántica,* Op. 3, based on "El Vito." By no means does he rely totally on borrowed material, but he does seem to employ it more than do his famous contemporaries.[29]

Ex. 6. Turina, "Petenera"/32–53. © 1913 Rouart Lerolle. Used by permission.

Many of Turina's melodies have a modal flavor, which results primarily from emphasis on the dominant by way of a Phrygian cadence. This modal quality, found in a great deal of Spanish music, is often referred to as "the Spanish idiom." Gilbert Chase offers a welcome clarification of this term when he states:

It is only when we specify "Andalusian," "Basque," "Asturian," or "Catalan" that we designate a definite musical idiom.

What has happened in actual practice is that the preponderance of the Andalusian idiom, with its semi-oriental exoticism, has tended to overshadow every other phase of Iberian popular music and to impress itself upon the world as the typical music of Spain.[30]

Turina's melodies are steeped in the Andalusian idiom, which "became a passport to international success for him."[31] What makes an Andalusian melody unique? What gives it its special attraction, an attraction that greatly influenced Turina's noted French contemporaries, Debussy and Ravel? For a start, it is difficult to come to grips with an Andalusian melody in terms of our major or minor modes because of its general movement within a system of interchangeable tetrachords. The more common terminology of "minor–major," used to indicate a mixture of modes, does not seem adequate to reflect the flexible character of an Andalusian scale. As Ex. 7 shows, this flexibility makes the second, third, sixth, and seventh degrees of the scale interchangeable major–minor degrees. This scalar trait, indigenous to the Andalusian idiom, places it in a peculiar harmonic–melodic position that, if not singled out at a specific moment for analysis, distorts the actual nature of the music.[32]

Ex. 7

Dean's assessment of Turina's harmonic style is most perceptive: "Throughout his entire output, the modal Spanish element jostles a Franckian luxuriance in such chords as the unresolved dominant ninth, and both alternate with patches of whole-tone colouring and unrelated triads which owe their existence to Debussy."[33] Although there were many harmonic innovations during Turina's compositional career—the tone clusters of Bartók, the quartal writing of Hindemith, the atonal and serial writing of Schönberg, the "tonality by assertion" of Stravinsky—Turina, unlike his colleague Falla, incorporated only the new French harmonies of Impressionism, while holding fast to the Romantic tradition.

Cyclical writing is the most salient feature of Turina's form. The emphasis on interrelated melodies stems from the post-Franckian atmosphere of the Schola Cantorum, where Turina studied with d'Indy. Exx. 8, 9, and 10 illustrate his exquisite and varied treatment of a lyrical melody as it recurs throughout *Sanlúcar de Barrameda,* Op. 24, his large, descriptive sonata.[34] Ex. 8 shows the first statement of this haunting theme (mm. 46–53)—hushed, simple, and direct. Ex. 9, from the third movement, shows the theme in open-fifth sonorities in the middle register of the piano and accompanied by delicate broken octaves in a higher register. For the climactic conclusion of the sonata (fourth movement), Turina employs the same theme embellished with a brilliant seven-note accompaniment figure that emits a broad sweeping effect (Ex. 10).

Ex. 8. Turina, *Sanlúcar de Barrameda*/i/39–53. © 1971. Used by permission of the publisher, Union Musical Española.

By no stretch of the imagination does Turina have an *Iberia* or a *Goyescas* in his output, but he did leave some large, technically demanding works as well as many gems in miniature. On the

Ex. 9.   Turina, *Sanlúcar de Barrameda*/iii/46–49. © 1971. Used by permission of the publisher, Union Musical Española.

Ex. 10.   Turina, *Sanlúcar de Barrameda*/iv/153–161. © 1971. Used by permission of the publisher, Union Musical Española.

whole, he seemed to be more at home using the training he received in Paris to paint a thousand scenes from his homeland. The intimate nature of his music exhibits a delightful balance between the sentimental and the gracious. Sopeña best sums up his style with the term *andalucismo universalizado,* meaning the union of traditional European forms with the spirit of Turina's native Andalusia.

Federico Mompou

FEDERICO MOMPOU (b. 1893), a native of Barcelona, began his studies at the Conservatory of the Liceo de Barcelona with Pedro Serra. At age eighteen he transferred to Paris to expand his studies under the direction of Isidore Philipp (piano), Ferdinand Motte Lacroix (piano), and Marcel Samuel Rousseau (harmony and composition).

With the outbreak of World War I, Mompou moved back to Barcelona, where he composed his first works for piano. He created his own individual style of music, breaking away from bar lines, key signatures, and traditional cadences. Mompou describes his music by the term *primitivista* — a path toward simplicity and synthesis to achieve maximal expression with minimal means.

In 1921, Mompou returned to Paris, where the noted critic Emile Vuillermoz listened to his music. As a result of a long article in which Vuillermoz praised Mompou's work, the composer soon received international acclaim. Mompou remained in Paris for the next twenty years, during which he composed many of his important works for piano. In 1941, he returned to Spain, reestablished permanent residence in his native Barcelona, and continued to work on vocal and choral compositions as well as various other pieces for piano.[35]

Mompou's music for piano represents one of the largest and most important collections for the instrument to come from Spain in this century. From the earliest to the most recent, it shows a remarkable consistency of style. In the words of Joanne Huot, "Mompou's music is rooted in an eclectic style, and in this he is perhaps closest to Manuel de Falla, who like Debussy was more his own personal guide. . . . The Andalusian art of Falla and the Catalan art of Mompou have evolved into perhaps the most original styles of contemporary Spanish music.''[36] Wilfrid Mellers once referred to Mompou as the only living Spanish composer to reveal the reality of Spain rather than the picture-postcard version and to be the creator of what could be the most narrowly limited stylization in musical history.[37]

According to Vuillermoz, "There have never been any true Debussians in France. The only disciple to continue for the composer of *La Mer* whom one would have the right to cite is perhaps the young Spaniard Federico Mompou. Mompou, who, without ever having known Debussy, has gathered up and comprehended the essentials of his teachings.''[38] Mompou's harmony is decidedly Impressionistic, though the notes at times are very sparse. He uses added seconds and sixths, with higher chromatic discords exploiting the piano's overtones. Though the harmonies suggest Debussy, the simple but effective melodies and the economy suggest the influence of Satie and the cult of the "enfantine.''[39]

Many of the interesting textures in Mompou's piano music are the direct result of the particular anatomy of his own hand. He likes to apply widely spaced open intervals and extensions of tenths, which his own fingers encompass without the least physical difficulty.[40]

Mompou's most characteristic works for piano are impregnated with Catalan folk ideas. He has indicated three divisions in his works: (1) those that depict subjectively the atmosphere and essence of the rural landscape of Catalonia as contrasted with the bustling life of the city of Barcelona (*Suburbis, Scènes d'Enfants,* and *Fêtes Lointaines*); (2) pieces inspired by the hidden and primitive enchantment of nature (*Charmes, Cants màgics,* and *Música callada*); and (3) works that stress the folklore element that underlies Catalan life (*Canción y Danza* series).[41]

Many of Mompou's piano works abandon bar lines completely or use them sparingly, but the rhythm does not become vague. One such example is *Cants màgics* ("Magic Chants"), Mompou's first published work, written between 1917 and 1919. Ex. 11 shows the

Ex. 11.   Mompou, *Cants màgics*/opening section. © 1930. Used by permission of the publisher, Union Musical Española.

typical widely spaced sonorities, a salient characteristic of Mompou's style. Adolfo Salazar was the first to proclaim the genius of Mompou in *El Sol* (Madrid). On June 18, 1921, after hearing *Cants màgics,* he wrote that Mompou's style resembled the slenderest of Debussy's preludes, though technically Mompou was nearer to Satie. Vuillermoz also praised him: "This young Spaniard, who works silently in his country retreat, is a magician. He searches in music for enchantments and spells wherewith to compound his magic songs. His formulas are short, concise, concentrated, but they possess a weird, hallucinating power of evocation."[42]

Some of Mompou's best-known piano works come from the series *Canción y Danza* ("Song and Dance").[43] Mompou states that he combined songs and dances in this series because of the contrast between the lyrical and the rhythmical. The pieces are written over a period of sixty years, and in one sense, they are quite similar and consistent in style; yet they undergo a gradual evolution from the early to the later ones, becoming increasingly austere and introspective. Many employ Catalonian folk songs.[44]

Ex. 12 shows Mompou's poetic use of a folk song, distributed on three staves, in *Canción* No. 2. The melody of "La senyora Isabel" appears in unison at a distance of two octaves with a hypnotic accompaniment sandwiched in between.

Ex. 12. Mompou, *Canción* No. 2. © 1926. Used by permission of the publisher, Union Musical Española.

Mompou always takes great care to "voice" his music clearly. Consequently, when he features the melody in the tenor register of the piano, the effect is often breathtaking. See Ex. 13 from *Canción No. 9*, based on the folksong "El Rossinyol."

Ex. 13. Mompou, *Canción No. 9*/12–23. © 1957 Editions Salabert. Used by permission.

Mompou's longest and most difficult work for piano is the *Variations sur un thème de Chopin,* based on Chopin's brief Prelude No. 7 in A major. Mompou does not adhere strictly to the ternary rhythm of the Prelude, but uses compound duple and simple duple meters as well for some variations. He incorporates a variation for left hand alone (No. 3), a mazurka (No. 5), a waltz (No. 9), and a galop (No. 12). Variation No. 10 even includes an excerpt from the middle section of Chopin's *Fantaisie Impromptu*. Mompou builds to a stunning climax in the virtuosic twelfth variation and concludes the work with a quiet epilogue.

Mompou says, "I always endeavor to make good music. My only aspiration is to write works that contain neither too little nor too much. . . . Some people find it difficult to understand that I don't have the same feel for grandiose form and traditional characteristics that they do; for me, nothing exists except *my* form and *my* concept."[45] This postulate seems to be the composer's dictum in all his works, but especially in *Música callada* ("Silent Music").

The four volumes of *Música callada* contain 28 pieces written between 1959 and 1967. Mompou takes his inspiration for these works from a statement made by the mystic poet San Juan de la Cruz, "La musica callada, la soledad sonora"—the concept of a music that would be the very voice of silence.[46] These intimate, abstract works, which Mompou at first did not intend to publish, are the quintessence of his later style for piano. They relate somewhat to the earlier *Cants màgics* and *Charmes,* but, as Mompou states, *Música callada* is more intellectual, more cerebral, more "composed."[47]

Mompou's piano works, on the whole, do not call for a virtuosic technique. More the difficulties "reside above all in the expression and poetry, and in understanding the harmonic structure—a musical intuition to discern the original harmonies in order to draw them out from those that are secondary, and to operate with the pedals the sonorities and resonances of the music is needed. It is an extremely plastic music that only very educated hands and fingers follow."[48] Walter Starkie summarizes Mompou's place in the twentieth century when he declares that Mompou's music is "art in miniature and comes as a pleasing relief in an age when we have grown weary of the immense and the gigantic and long to see the universe reflected in a single drop of water."[49]

The Grupo de los Ocho

In the spring of 1930, a group of young composers banded together in Madrid and became known as the Grupo de los Ocho. It counted among its members Juan José Mantecón, Salvador Bacarisse, Fernando Remacha, Rodolfo Halffter, Julian Bautista, Ernesto Halffter, Gustavo Pittaluga, and Rosa García Ascot. All made significant contributions to Spanish piano music, except García Ascot (b. 1906), the sole female of the group. Her only contribution was a suite for piano. She later settled in Mexico.

JUAN JOSÉ MANTECÓN (b. 1896), of Pontevedra, was the oldest member of the Grupo de los Ocho and was primarily a writer on music rather than a composer. His piano works include *Capa de pasos, Españolada,* and *Dos sonatinas.*

SALVADOR BACARISSE (b. 1898), of Madrid, studied piano with Antonio Alberdí and composition with Conrado del Campo at the Madrid Conservatory. He won several national prizes, notably for the symphonic poem *La Nave de Ulise* in 1921 and for *Música sinfónica* in 1931. He was also awarded the National Prize in 1934 "for the merit of his work as a whole." From 1925 to 1936 he was musical director of the radio station Unión Radio in Madrid. After the Spanish Civil War, Bacarisse left Spain.

For the piano, he has written *Siete variaciones sobre un tema de las canciones del marqués de Santillana; Veinticuatro preludios; Berceuse; Pasodoble; Preludio, fugueta y rondó; Tema con variaciones; Toccata;* and *Cinco piezas breves. Heraldos,* symphonic impressions, is also available in a piano version, but proves difficult to negotiate. The *Toccata* contains interesting bitonal writing but difficult passages in thirds and chords of the octave and sixth.

FERNANDO REMACHA (b. 1898), of Tudela, studied violin in Pamplona and Madrid. He also studied composition with Conrado del Campo. Later, on a scholarship, he worked with Gian Francesco Malipiero in Rome and won the National Prize with his string quartet.

Remacha's *Tres piezas* for piano deserve special mention. Though "Spanish" in flavor, they are not the usual description of some regional locale. The first piece, *Allegro,* mostly in 5/4 meter, displays a hypnotic ostinato with downward cascading figures. The second, *Lento,* features the rhythm of the *habanera* with harmonic planing of the Impressionist school. *Con alegría,* the last and most difficult movement, contains hand-crossings, cadenzas in fifths, and exquisite writing on three staves. These works certainly merit further investigation by pianists. Remacha has also written a Sonatina for piano.

RODOLFO HALFFTER (b. 1900), brother of Ernesto Halffter, is a composer of German-Spanish parentage. During the Spanish Civil War, R. Halffter was chief of the music section of the Ministry of Propaganda with the Loyalist government. After its defeat, he fled to France and eventually to Mexico, where he settled in 1939 and became a naturalized citizen in 1940. Halffter has been largely self-taught, but he profited from the valuable advice of Manuel de Falla.

In Mexico, Halffter founded a progressive triannual periodical, *Nuestra Música*. He has also been professor of musical analysis and music history at the National Conservatory, director of the publishing firm Ediciones Mexicanas, and music critic for *El Universal Gráfico*.

R. Halffter's piano music can be divided into two distinct periods: polytonal (through 1951) and serial (beginning in 1953). The pre-serial works for piano include *Dos sonatas de El Escorial,* Op. 2; *Preludio y Fuga,* Op. 4; *Danza de Avila,* Op. 9; *Homenaje a Antonio Machado,* Op. 13; *Primera Sonata,* Op. 16; *Once Bagatelas,* Op. 19; and *Segunda Sonata,* Op. 20.[50]

We have a clue to the style and form of *Dos sonatas de El Escorial,* Op. 2, from part of the title. The Escorial is a monastery outside Madrid built by Philip II between 1562 and 1586. Every autumn, after 1733, Scarlatti resided there with the royal family;[51] and Antonio Soler, a pupil of Scarlatti, took Holy Orders and entered the monastery of the Escorial, to spend the rest of his life there as a composer, organist, and choirmaster. The very spirit and structure of Soler's many sonatas betray him as a disciple of Scarlatti. Thus, we may conclude that in *Dos sonatas de El Escorial,* Halffter is trying to reflect the spirit of these two great masters. His harmonic vocabulary, however, is the piquant bitonal language of the modern period.[52]

Both sonatas of Op. 2 are in a bipartite structure, as in a Scarlatti model. The same is true for *Danza de Avila,* Op. 9, a work with a folk-dance rhythm, characterized by hemiola, that is cast in the form of a Scarlatti sonata. The structure used in the first Escorial sonata and in *Danza de Avila* is so close to Scarlatti/Soler that one can easily detect Kirkpatrick's crux. However, in the second sonata, Halffter prefers to recapitulate, in an abridged manner, the opening material in the key of the dominant, after an eight-measure excursion in the minor dominant. This procedure closely resembles the embryonic sonata form of the finale to Haydn's Sonata in A major (No. 12 in the Päsler edition, No. 28 in the Zilcher edition), though Haydn recapitulates in the tonic after a seven-measure excursion. Nonetheless, the style, spirit, and rhythmic drive of the Halffter work are unmistakably more related to Scarlatti.[53]

The attractive *Homenaje a Antonio Machado*, Op. 13, in honor of the Spanish poet Antonio Machado, contains four movements, each prefaced by lines of poetry. The outer movements are longer and faster, the middle movements slower. The Hispanism of Halffter is readily apparent here, be it in slow or fast movements.

Halffter's first major sonata, Op. 16, is in three compact movements—the first in sonata form, the second a slow imitative movement, and the third a bustling rondo. The outer, fast movements feature Halffter's typical rhythmic complexities, that of grouping notes across the bar line. Michael Field found the slow movement a good example of creating a penetrating emotion by very simple means, employing Halffter's method of "seventh-chord polytonality."[54] The finale features passages of bitonality with different key signatures for the treble and bass clefs. According to one reviewer, "The whole work is beautifully written, unpretentious and a pleasure to the ear."[55]

Once bagatelas ("Eleven Bagatelles"), Op. 19, is most likely a pedagogical work, written to initiate the student in the problems of modern music: polytonality, the combination of opposing rhythms, and neo-modality.[56] Nos. 4, 9, and 11 are especially effective, showing the clear crystalline piano style of Halffter (see Ex. 14).

Segunda Sonata, Op. 20, dedicated to Carlos Chávez, is laid out in Classical construction with four movements: *Allegro*, in sonata–allegro form; *Andante poco mosso*, in song form; a scherzo and trio; and the finale, a rondo.[57] The first theme of the slow movement is one of Halffter's most poignant lyrical utterances (see Ex. 15). Note the characteristic sevenths formed with the bass.

Michael Field contends that the chord of the seventh is the

Ex. 14.   Halffter, *Bagatelle No. 11/1–10.* © 1962. Used by permission of the publisher, Union Musical Española.

pivotal point of Halffter's harmonic structure and that by it he is strongly linked to Falla and the Spanish tradition. He explains it in the following manner. The very first chord of Falla's Concerto for harpsichord, flute, oboe, clarinet, violin, and violoncello

is the keystone in the structure of Falla's later music and that of his legitimate successor, Rodolfo Halffter. It consists of a clash between the seventh chord of the tonic E-flat minor, combined with the chord of D major. The resultant phenomenon is what Falla always referred to as "apparent polytonality," for the notes of the chord of D major are, in fact, the natural harmonic resonances of the notes of the seventh chord on E-flat. The minor mode is used to provide a common note between the two chords (F-sharp or G-flat). This is not arbitrary chromatic altera-tion and constitutes a principle from which Falla, and Halffter

Ex. 15. R. Halffter, *Segunda Sonata para Piano*, Op. 20/ii/1–9.
Copyright 1955 by Rodolfo Halffter. Sole selling agent Southern Music
Publishing Co. Inc. Used by permission. All rights reserved.

after him, built up a harmonic system capable of great force and
evocative power.[58]

According to Gilbert Chase, R. Halffter is more cerebral in his
conceptions than his brother. R. Halffter at first showed influences
of Schönberg and, though he subsequently moved toward more
tonal clarity, he retained a mordant and ironic quality reminiscent
of Stravinsky's middle period.[59]

JULIAN BAUTISTA (1901–1961), born in Madrid, studied

composition with Conrado del Campo at the Madrid Conservatory. He won the National Prize in 1923 for his String Quartet No. 1 and in 1926 for String Quartet No. 2; and in 1933, he won first prize for his *Obertura para una Opera Grotesca* in the International Competition sponsored by Unión Radio. In 1936 Bautista was appointed professor of harmony at the Madrid Conservatory. After the Civil War, during which many of his manuscripts were destroyed, he left Spain for Belgium and then Argentina, where he became active in the Argentine League of Composers.

The Argentine critic Roberto Garcia Morillo suggests that four different "manners" may be discerned in Bautista's music: Impressionistic, nationalist, neoclassical, and contemporary.[60] According to Chase, *Colores,* for piano, reveals a modernism divorced from any deliberate nationalism.[61] However, *Preludio y Danza,* for piano, is a decidedly nationalist piece of the Andalusian variety. The biting dissonances, vital rhythms, and guitar effects make for a very exciting work. Especially to be noted are the rhythmic patterns written "across the bar lines" in the dance movement.

ERNESTO HALFFTER (b. 1905), brother of Rodolfo Halffter, was born in Madrid. He showed musical talent at an early age and eventually attracted the attention of Manuel de Falla, who took him as a private pupil. In 1925, Halffter won a National Prize for his *Sinfonietta* in D major, a work fashioned after the Classical sinfonia concertante. Three years later, his one-act ballet *Sonatina,* based on a poem by Rubén Darío, was produced in Paris.

Halffter became conductor of the Orquesta Bética of Seville in 1924 and director of the National Conservatory of Seville in 1934, holding this post until the outbreak of the Civil War in 1936. He later settled in Lisbon. His early works for solo piano include *Marche joyeuse,* three sonatas, *Pregón, Habanera, Llanto por Ricardo Viñes,* and transcriptions from the ballet *Sonatina:* "Danza de la Pastora," "Danza de la Gitana," and "Las Doncellas," a suite of dances.

Marche joyeuse, dedicated to Adolfo Salazar, is crisp, biting, and bitonal. In general, it shows witty, effective writing for the piano, though the surprise whole-tone ending seems a bit abrupt. Supposedly Halffter was greatly influenced by Debussy's *L'Isle joyeuse* when he composed this work.[62]

His three sonatas, according to Salazar, are "Scarlattian in aspect, but modern in spirit."[63] Though the Sonata in D major features some attractive bitonal writing, many passages are somewhat unidiomatic for keyboard, more orchestral.

Pregón, reflecting the spirit of Cuba, is based on an alluring rhythmic pattern in 5/8: ♪♩ ♩♪♩ . The tonality is F-sharp major with delightful tinges of dissonance and the usual characteristic Phrygian implications.

Llanto por Ricardo Viñes is one of E. Halffter's most inspired works for piano. Along with works by Rodrigo and Mompou, it was originally part of a collected memorial to the great Spanish pianist Ricardo Viñes, who played numerous new works by his contemporaries. The depth and profundity of Halffter's work comes through immediately. One can hear the Falla of *Homenaje a Dukas* quite clearly in the many arpeggiated passages, the effective use of grace notes, the exquisite voicing, and the overall stark severity of the work. Through this piece, one can easily see Halffter's compositions as successors to the late works of Falla.

Halffter's transcriptions for piano have become as popular if not more so than his original works for piano, a fact also true of Falla's works. *Danza de la Pastora* and *Danza de la Gitana,* both from the ballet *Sonatina,* are excellent examples of this composer's clear, crystalline craftsmanship. They are quite effective as piano solos in their own right, and the folk-dance atmosphere gives them immediate appeal.

GUSTAVO PITTALUGA (b. 1906), of Madrid, studied at the University of Madrid. While preparing himself for a legal and diplomatic career, he also studied music; he was a composition student of Oscar Esplá.[64]

As a member of the Grupo de los Ocho, Pittaluga took it upon himself to define the point of view of his comrades in a lecture, later printed in *La Gaceta Literaria*.[65] The article significantly does not discuss nationalism or folklorism, with which musicians of the previous generation had been so largely preoccupied. Instead it stresses the necessity of creating "authentic" music of an entirely nonethnic variety, that is, music whose worth should be measured solely by its *musical* qualities, without literary, philosophical, or metaphysical associations. It called for "no Romanticism, no chromaticism, no divagations, and no chords of the diminished seventh."[66]

Pittaluga's piano works include *Trois pièces pour une espagnolade, Six danse espagnolade en suite, Homenaje a Mateo Albéniz* (originally for guitar, arranged by the composer for piano), and *Hommage pour le tombeau de Manuel de Falla* (for harpsichord or piano).

Others from Madrid

VICENTE ARREGUI (1871–1925) studied at the Madrid Conservatory, where he won first prize in piano and composition. In 1902 he went on to Paris and Rome for further study. Later he became music critic for *El Debate* in Madrid. Arregui composed operas, symphonic works, and for piano *Tres piezas líricas, Impresiones populares,* and Sonata in F minor.

The Sonata is Arregui's *tour de force* for keyboard. It is a long, difficult work in three movements and is one of the few large-scale sonatas by a Spanish composer from the first quarter of the century. The first movement, *Lento y triste a modo de marcha funebre,* opens with a theme based on the descending minor tetrachord, a very familiar "Spanish" motive. This idea is contrasted with a more dramatic second theme in F-sharp minor, accompanied by orchestral tremolo effects (see Ex. 16). After a brief interlude, there occurs a reverse recapitulation, with the second theme followed by a hint at the opening material.

The second movement, in F major, *Allegro molto scherzando,* proves to be a grandiose scherzo and trio. The principal scherzo

Ex. 16. Arregui, Sonata in F minor/i/38–40.

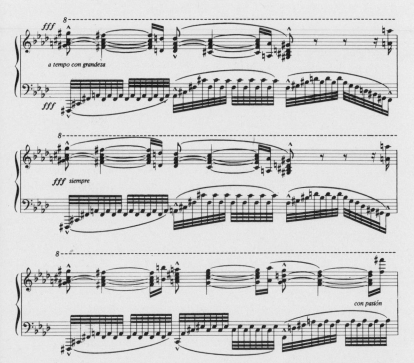

idea is a light, scampering, staccato theme, featuring added tones and ninth chords, while the trio section exhibits a broad expansive theme. The whole movement is very difficult technically, and a bit long and tedious.

The virtuosic finale, in C minor, *Allegro assai con fuoco,* is also cast in sonata–allegro form, but displays more development of thematic material than does the first movement. The opening section is mostly figural in style, while the second theme, in the key of the subdominant, is very expressive, with an undulating triplet accompaniment. There follows a demanding development section with a recapitulation that is obscured, the exact opening material being omitted. This time Arregui places the second theme in the key of the submediant. To conclude the work, he writes a coda with fast, brilliant figuration that climaxes to a Lisztian recitative passage. Even the final chords of the tonic, submediant in first inversion, tonic smack of Liszt.

CONRADO DEL CAMPO (1879–1953), violist and composer, studied at the Madrid Conservatory, where he later became a professor of harmony and composition. He had a profound influence on the musical life of Madrid and, as a teacher, turned out some of the most outstanding musicians in Spain in this century.[67]

Conrado del Campo came first under the influence of Franck, then Richard Strauss. In the words of Adolfo Salazar, "Chromaticism, national lyric drama, and *Sturm und Drang* are the terms that define the personality of Conrado del Campo from his youth to his maturity."[68] The orchestra and string quartet were his favorite modes of expression.

According to Salazar, the fact that Conrado del Campo was not a pianist and did not intend to write for piano had two consequences: It made it difficult for his music to become known, and it resulted in an aversion on his part toward the Impressionistic tendencies, which came from the piano, the easiest medium for experimentation.[69] But eventually he did write *Paisajes de Granada, Impresión castellana,* and *Añoranza* for solo piano and *Rondel* for two pianos.

JULIO GÓMEZ (1886–1973), composer and music critic, studied piano, theory, and composition at the Madrid Conservatory in addition to receiving a Ph.D. His research topic involved Blas de Laserna, a noted eighteenth-century Spanish composer of *tonadillas.*[70] Gómez later became the director of the Museo Arqueológico of Toledo, worked in the music division of the Biblioteca Nacional in Madrid, and was music librarian at the library of the Madrid Conservatory. Though he is known mostly for his orchestral, theater, and vocal literature, he did write *Variaciones sobre un tema salamantino* for piano.

MANUEL MARTÍNEZ CHUMILLAS (b. 1902), an architect and composer, has written three piano works: *Tres piezas de aire popular flamenco, Letargo,* and *Cinco sonoridades,* all characteristic of his musical endeavors.

JAVIER ALFONSO (b. 1905) studied at the Madrid Conservatory with José Tragó, Pérez Casas, and Conrado del Campo, as well as in Paris with José Iturbi and Alfred Cortot. Later he became a professor of piano at the Madrid Conservatory. For many years, he concertized in the principal cities of Europe and America, and in 1946 he was awarded the National Prize in piano. Among his piano compositions are Sonata in G minor, *Scherzo, Seis sonetos* (homenaje a Góngora), *Los peregrinos pasan, Capricho en forma de Bolero, Guajira, Nana, Díptico* (homenaje a Turina), *Seis piezas infantiles, Preludio y Toccata, Impromptu,* and *Suite* (homenaje a Isaac Albéniz). He has also written *Ensayo sobre la técnica trascendente del piano.*

The Suite in memory of Albéniz, a more recent work, shows a variety of styles. The opening movement, "Ofrenda," exhibits tinges of Impressionism, while the interesting second movement, "Estudio para el empleo de sonoridades simultáneas," shows various patterns and scales in minor seconds. The most novel feature of the third movement, "Gesto," is the plucking of certain notes inside the piano. The fourth movement, "Impromptu," is another study in minor seconds but of a "perpetual motion" variety. The finale, "Danza," returns to the more Andalusian atmosphere, as in the first movement, but in the style of a dance.

Cataluña

JULI GARRETA (1875–1925), a Catalan composer from San Feliu de Guixols, received a few music lessons from his father, a watchmaker and musician, but for the most part he was self-taught. Garreta played violin in a small orchestra and eventually became the pianist/director of a quintet. He composed mostly *sardanas* and orchestral works, with some chamber pieces and songs.

His only composition for piano is the large Sonata in C minor, which received its premier performance in 1923. It even attracted

the attention of Blanche Selva and Fanny Davies, who performed it
in Paris and London, respectively. The sonata has four large
movements, basically a Classical conception, but the harmonic language shifts between Wagner and Debussy. All verbal expressive
marks in the score are in Catalan.

The first movement opens with a fantasylike introduction (tonic
and dominant statements); the main theme, a very pianistic figura-
tive idea, does not begin until measure 47. A contrasting lyrical
theme, in the remote key of A major, is based on a descending
scale pattern. The development section expands many of the
former motives and is followed by an abbreviated recapitulation in
the tonic minor. Portions of the introductory material also return,
but the second theme has been omitted.

The second movement, *Poc a poc* (slowly), should be performed
in the manner of a fantasia. This ternary movement is very
chromatic, contains several changes of time signature, and exhibits
numerous sweeping figures and arabesques.

The third movement, normally a scherzo, turns out to be a *sardana*, the national dance of Cataluña. It is not surprising to find it
here, for Garreta wrote so many of these dances he was known as
the "Wagner of the Sardana."[71]

The finale also begins with a fantasylike introduction, this time
written on three staves. On the whole, this movement has many
more "Classical" passages, somewhat reminiscent of Beethoven
(see Ex. 17). The first theme is bold and syncopated. After many
measures, Garreta arrives at a lyrical theme in E-flat major. The
development section is quite extended, with an unfolding of
numerous motives heard before, and the work concludes with an
abbreviated recapitulation in the tonic.

Along with Turina's picturesque sonata, *Sanlúcar de Barrameda,*
Op. 24, Garreta's Sonata in C minor represents one of the best in
the genre to come from Spain in the first quarter of the twentieth
century. Pablo Casals, who was very instrumental in getting Garreta's works performed, described the composer as a "brilliant man
and profoundly intuitive."[72]

JAIME PAHISSA (b. 1880), of Barcelona, was Enric Morera's

Ex. 17. Garreta, Sonata in C minor/iv/33–40. © Union Musical Española, n.d. Used by permission of the publisher.

most important pupil. Pahissa studied both music and architecture at the University of Barcelona, but finally decided on music for a career. He became a leading figure in Catalan musical life, but in 1937 he moved to Argentina, where as pedagogue, composer, and orchestra director, he exercised a great influence on the artistic media.

According to Gilbert Chase,

> Pahissa cultivates a "vertical" or "linear" style of writing in which harmony plays a secondary role. He considers himself the inventor of a "system of pure dissonance" which is neither tonal, nor atonal, nor polytonal. His *Suite Intertonal* for orchestra was written to illustrate this system. Another orchestral work, *Monodia*, is intended to demonstrate that a composition can be based exclusively on melody, without regard to harmony or rhythm.[73]

However, most of his music does not evidence these experimental practices.

Pahissa is mostly known for his larger works, operatic and orchestral, but he has written the following pieces for piano: *Seis pequeñas fugas a tres voces*, *Preludio y grandes fugas a dos voces*, *Escenas catalanas*, *Piezas espirituales*, *Nit de somnis*, *Dos danzas catalanas*, and a Sonata.

JOAN MANÉN (b. 1883), a Catalan violinist and composer from Barcelona, showed unusual musical ability as a child. By age seven, he was performing Chopin and Bach in public. Manén studied both violin and piano, but preferred the violin. He wrote a suite for piano entitled *Cuadros*, and his style essentially follows the tradition of Wagner and Richard Strauss.[74]

BALTASAR SAMPER (b. 1888), of Palma de Mallorca, settled in Barcelona, where he studied piano with Granados and composition with Pedrell. Under the guidance of Pedrell, Samper became interested in the folk music of his native Mallorca and set about collecting Balearic melodies. He also enjoyed great success as a concert pianist. Later he moved to Mexico, where he became director of the Mexican Archive of Folklore. Samper's works for piano include *Balada, Variaciones,* and *Danzas mallorquinas.*

GASPAR CASSADÓ (1897–1966), of Barcelona, son of the well-known organist/composer Joaquín Cassadó, began his music studies at age five. At age seven, he began cello lessons and two years later gave a concert that was so well received that he was given a scholarship to study further. In 1910, he became a student of Casals in Paris. Under the influence of Falla and Ravel, he began composing, but with the outbreak of World War I, he returned to Barcelona to study composition with his father. Cassadó eventually became one of the most outstanding cellists from Spain and toured extensively. Later he became a professor at the Accademia Musicale Chigiana at Siena, Italy.

Though mostly known as a virtuoso cellist and composer-transcriber of cello music, Cassadó wrote *Quatre pièces espagnoles* and *Sonata breve* for piano. *Sonata breve* gives evidence of fine craft. It is in three movements and reveals Cassadó's Impressionistic tendencies, emphasizing quartal writing. The first movement (Proemio), an abridged sonata–allegro form, contains subtle Spanish inflections. It ends on a suspensive chord, and the composer directs that this movement lead directly into the next. The second movement (scherzo) is delightful and witty, with the main theme marked "quasi burlesco." Although the meter is 3/8, most of the patterns are grouped in pairs "across the bar line." The Spanish element can also be found here. The concluding rondo opens with an expressive folklike theme and is contrasted with more rapid arabesques and chordal patterns between the hands.

ROBERTO GERHARD (1896–1970), born in Valls, Tarragona, studied piano with Granados and composition with Pedrell. Gerhard was Pedrell's last pupil. Afterward he worked with Schönberg in Vienna and Berlin from 1923 until 1928. He subsequently held a brief professorship at the Escola Normal de la Generalitat in Barcelona and served in the music division of the Biblioteca de Cataluña. After the defeat of the Republic in the Spanish Civil War, he settled in Cambridge, England, where he made his living almost entirely as a free-lance composer. He was visiting professor of composition at the University of Michigan during the spring of 1960 and at the Berkshire Music Center, Tanglewood, during the summer of 1961. In recent years, he showed interest in electronic music.

Though Gerhard's piano works are relatively insignificant when compared to his orchestral and chamber works, they are mentioned here because of the stature of the composer. They are *Dos apunts, Soirées de Barcelone* (arranged from the orchestral suites), *Don Quixote,* ballet and dances from *Don Quixote,* and *Tres impromptus.*

MANUEL BLANCAFORT (b. 1897), of La Garriga, was the son of a pianist, who gave him his first musical instruction. Blancafort then worked with Lamote de Grignon. Like Mompou in the early twentieth century, Blancafort represented the Spanish Anti-Wagnerism in Paris, and came under the spell of Impressionism. Later, he was more influenced by Les Six and Stravinsky.

Blancafort, like Mompou, has been one of the most important Catalan composers of piano music. His output contains *Notas de antaño, Juegos y danzas, Canciones de montaña, Cants intims, El parque de atracciones, Polca del equilibrista, Chemins, American souvenir, Sonatina antigua, Dos nocturnos, Romanza intermedio y marcha, Momentos musicales, Tres tonadas,* and *Piezas espirituales.*

The pianist Ricardo Viñes introduced *El parque de atracciones* to the French public, establishing Blancafort as a representative of the modern Spanish school.[75] The four pieces entitled *Chemins,* · dedicated to Mompou, are good examples of Blancafort's Impressionistic writing. Unpretentious, but very delightful, these small works show an excellent command of harmony, as liberated by Debussy and Ravel. Both slow and fast movements prove attractive.

JAIME MÁS PORCEL (b. 1909), pianist and composer from Palma de Mallorca, obtained a scholarship in 1927 from the Diputación de Baleares that permitted him to study with José Tragó in

Madrid. He was given an additional scholarship to continue his studies in Paris, and there he worked with Alfred Cortot. He was mostly known as a teacher of piano and as a concert artist. His few piano compositions include *Suite mallorquina,* six Sonatinas, and *Méteores.*

JOSÉ ARDÉVOL (b. 1911), son of the Catalan pianist Fernando Ardévol, completed his musical training with his father. At the age of nineteen he went to Havana, Cuba, to become maestro for a Jesuit college. In 1934, he founded the Orquesta da Cámara in Havana and became its director. His music has been described as almost always modal, contrapuntal, and diatonic.[76]

Ardévol has written numerous works for orchestra, voices, films, chamber groups, and the following pieces for piano: *Capriccio, Nocturnos, Invenciones a dos voces, Preludios, Sonatina,* and four Sonatas.

JOAN MASSIÀ (b. 1890), Catalan composer, studied piano and violin and eventually toured as a violinist with the famed pianist Blanche Selva. His piano works include *Ocell de Pedra, El gorg negre, Libellula,* and *Scherzo.*

AGUSTÍ GRAU (b. 1893) is important for his piano works, especially *Hores tristes.*[77] EUGENI BADIA (b. 1904) contributed an interesting *Sonata a l'antiga,* and JOSEP ROMA has written *Sonatina hierática.*

Valencia and the Levante

EDUARDO LÓPEZ-CHAVARRI (1875–1970) was at one time a very important leader of the Valencian school. He studied with Pedrell in Barcelona and became known as a composer, musicologist, and poet. López-Chavarri taught aesthetics and musicology at the Valencia Conservatory and also conducted the conservatory orchestra.

For piano he wrote *Cuentos y Fantasías* (which contains the popular "Leyenda del Castillo Moro"), *Feuille d'Album, Danzas valencianas,* and *Sonata Levantina.* The last-named, a work in four movements, evokes the folk music of the region known as Levante—Murcia and Alicante. The third movement (Minueto) and fourth movement (Fantasía) are especially attractive for their folk-dance tunes.

FRANCESCH CUESTA (1889–1921), a student of Salvador Giner, contributed some Valencian piano music during his short life. His piano works include *Danses Valenciennes, Sérénade Valencienne, Prélude et Improvisation, Chanson Valencienne,* and *Scènes d'enfants.* Henri Collet found his works to be delightful and poetic in nature.[78]

MANUEL PALAU (1893–1967), of Alfara del Patriarca, Valencia, studied piano and composition at the Conservatory of Valencia. To further his studies in music, he went to Paris, where he studied composition with Koechlin and Bertelin and received helpful advice and instruction on orchestration from Ravel. Meanwhile, he was a teaching assistant in aesthetics and music history as well as in the vocal and instrumental division of the Conservatory of Valencia.

Palau won the Spanish National Prize in music in 1927 and 1945. He directed several orchestras and choral groups in Madrid and Valencia, and was named director of the Conservatory of Valencia in 1952. His earliest works are based on elements of Mediterranean folklore. Later he embraced polytonality, atonality, and a modal style.[79]

Palau left a substantial addition to twentieth-century Spanish piano literature. His major works are *Valencia, Levantina, Sonatina Valenciana, Tres impresiones fugaces, Tocata en mi menor, Campanas, Paisaje Balear, Danza Hispalense, Danza Ibérica, Evocación de Andalucía,* and *Homenaje a Debussy.*[80]

Sonatina Valenciana shows the influence of Scarlatti, with its binary structure and pungent dissonances. Containing Valencian folklike melodies, it proves to be one of Palau's most desirable works. In sharp contrast to this work are the *Tres impresiones fugaces,* which reveal an appealing use of dissonance and bitonality.

Four attractive works that show the influence of French Impressionism are *Paisaje Balear, Campanas, Homenaje a Debussy,* and *Tocata en mi menor*. The *Tocata* is an exceptionally striking work, wholly pianistic, with a singing melody set off by a rippling accompaniment (see Ex. 18).

Ex. 18.   Palau, *Tocata en mi menor*/1–14. © 1946. Used by permission of the publisher, Union Musical Española.

According to Leon Tello, a decided change in style can be detected in *Danza Ibérica* and *Evocación de Andalucía,* which reflect "a distinct language, more concentrated and polished, more concise and compressed."[81]

JOSÉ MORENO GANS (b. 1897), of Algemesi, Valencia, studied composition with Conrado del Campo at the Madrid Conservatory, and after being awarded a scholarship by the Fundación Conde de Cartegena, furthered his studies in Vienna, Berlin, and Paris. For piano, he has written a Sonata, *Algemesienses, Gavota, Danza con variaciones, Pastoral,* and *Homenaje a Albéniz.*

The last work is a suite of three movements entitled "Sevillanas," "Saeta," and "Final." It reflects the Seville that inspired Albéniz's masterpieces, but represents a very conservative approach, even more so than Albéniz's works for his time.

JOAQUÍN RODRIGO was born in 1902 in Sagunto, Valencia, and was blind from the age of three. After studying in Valencia, he went on to Paris in 1927, where he studied with Paul Dukas and also profited from the advice of Manuel de Falla. Rodrigo returned to Spain in 1933 and was awarded a scholarship to continue his studies in Paris. In 1936, at the outbreak of the Civil War, he returned to his homeland; and in 1939 he took up residence in Madrid and won instant fame with his *Concierto de Aranjuez* for guitar and orchestra. In addition to being acclaimed as a composer, Rodrigo is also known as a critic and lecturer, having been a professor of music history at the University of Madrid.

Rodrigo has written numerous works for piano, some of which include *Suite, Preludio al gallo mañanero, Serenata española, Sonada de adiós (Homenaje a Paul Dukas), Danzas de españa, A l'ombre de Torre Bermeja (Homenaje a Ricardo Viñes), Seguidillas del diablo,* and *Cinco sonatas de Castilla con toccata a modo de pregón.*[82] Federico Sopeña cites the *Preludio al gallo mañanero* (1928) as one of Rodrigo's most ingenious piano pieces, a work that covers the keyboard from sub-contra A to A[4] with effervescence and intelligent abandon.[83]

A work of great pathos and depth is *Homenaje a Paul Dukas,* which was originally published in the musical supplement of *La Revue Musicale,* May–June 1936. Set in the difficult key of A-flat minor, it is a brief yet telling encounter with Rodrigo's craft. The composer sets a plaintive tune with a mesmerizing accompaniment, both of which are difficult to negotiate at times.

The *Sonatas de Castilla* (1952) show Rodrigo's penchant for minor seconds, which help to give his works a burlesque flavor. The "Sonata, como un Tiento," dedicated to Frank Marshall, is the most lyrical of the five.

Another Valencian composer is VICENTE ASENCIO (b. 1903), who wrote the following piano works: *Dos danzas, Giga, Infantívola, Cuatro danzas españolas,* Sonatina, and *Romancillo a Chopin.*

OSCAR ESPLÁ (1886–1976), of Alicante, at first prepared for a career in civil engineering and later received a doctorate in philosophy. He had little systematic instruction in music as a child, though he showed musical ability. Furthering his musical studies as a youth, he spent time in France, Italy, Belgium, and Germany, where he studied with Max Reger. In 1909 he won an international prize in Vienna with a suite for orchestra. By 1931, Esplá had become a figure of national importance in Spain. He became president of the Junta Nacional de Música and director of the Madrid Conservatory. During the Spanish Civil War, he settled in Brussels. In 1953, Esplá was elected to the Real Academia de Bellas Artes de San Fernando in Spain.

Many of Esplá's works are based on a scale that he derived from the folk music of his native region, the Levante, the region of Murcia and Alicante. The scale consists of the notes C, D-flat, E-flat, F-flat, G-flat, G-natural, A-flat, B-flat.[84]

Esplá, stated,

> I have constructed my works very openly on the basis of this scale, whose special color agrees with that of the folk songs of the Levante and with their own melodic–harmonic tendency; the bonds of tonic–dominant are related to that established in the diatonic scale; but, with the exception of the perfect chord, which can be constructed on the tonic, no exact equivalent exists between the harmonic links of the two scales.[85]

According to Henri Collet, Esplá first used this scale in the piano work *Evocaciones* (1918).[86] It is also used in *Crepúsculos, Ronda Levantina,* and "Canto de vendimia."[87] Ex. 19, from "Canto de vendimia" (first movement of the suite *La Sierra*), shows Esplá's use of the scale, transposed to F-sharp, G, A, B-flat, C, C-sharp, D, E. In the opinion of Salazar, the lack of definite tonal contrasts in the scale produces a certain monotony and uncertainty of construction in some of Esplá's works.[88]

Esplá supposedly did not believe in musical "nationalism" or in reproducing folk melodies to obtain local color. His musical system was to give "universal character" to his music. Unless one is thoroughly grounded in the music of Levante, Esplá's music will not sound "Spanish."[89] A good introduction to the music of his region

Ex. 19. Esplá, "Canto de vendimia"/1–9. © 1949. Used by permission of the publisher, Editions Max Eschig.

is *Levante,* ten pieces based on dance themes. They show mostly a modal flavor, but are quite a refreshing change from the universally known Andalusian types.

One of Esplá's larger, more difficult works for piano is *Sonata española,* Op. 53. This work was written at the invitation of UNESCO for the "Tombeau de Chopin," an international homage to Chopin celebrated in Paris in October 1949, on the centennial of his death.

The first movement is in sonata–allegro form with no development. Especially to be noted is the recapitulation, which features the plaintive main theme above a shimmering accompaniment. The second movement, "Mazurka on a popular theme," displays Esplá's whole-tone writing. The finale, also an abridged sonata form, contains some difficult, abstract writing, even breaking into three staves at times. Ex. 20 gives the principal theme of the movement, one of Esplá's captivating folklike melodies.

Ex. 20.   Esplá, *Sonata española*/iii/97–106. © 1952. Used by permission of the publisher, Union Musical Española.

RAFAEL RODRÍGUEZ ALBERT (b. 1902), was born in Alicante, but resides in Madrid. He was a pupil of Oscar Esplá and received advice in composition from Manuel de Falla. Rodríguez Albert has been lecturer, pianist, and teacher at the Colegio Nacional de Ciegos in Madrid. His piano works include *Impromptu, Preludio, Homenaje a Albéniz, Tres miniaturas, El cadáver del príncipe, Meditación de sigüenza, Homenaje a Falla, Cuatro preludios,* and Sonatina.

The Basque Region and Navarra

JOSÉ ANTONIO DE DONOSTIA (1886–1956), noted Basque musicologist and composer, was born in San Sebastián. He entered the Franciscan-Capuchin order in 1902. Padre Donostia studied harmony, counterpoint, fugue, and instrumentation in Paris, where he lived from 1920 to 1923. Later he made frequent trips to Paris to continue his contacts with French composers. For many years he was organist/choirmaster in Navarra, in the town of Lecaroz.

Though chiefly known for his work in musicology, especially in Basque folk music, Donostia wrote music for organ, voice, piano, chamber instruments, and chorus. A complete edition of his works in twelve volumes is in progress, ten volumes having been completed.[90] The piano music can be found in Volume 10 of the series.

Donostia's piano music is divided into three groups: *Preludios vascos, Mosaico,* and *Infantiles*. The first group, *Basque Preludes,* was written between 1912 and 1923 and includes such works as "Improvisación," "Diálogo," "Canción triste," and "Paisaje sulentino." Most of these pieces are of the Romantic salon type. The second group, *Mosaic* (1913–1954), contains several works for guitar transcribed for piano by the composer. A notable work here, originally for piano, is the "Homenaje a Juan Crisóstomo de Arriaga," in memory of the great Basque composer from the early nineteenth century. In this work, Donostia uses a Neoclassic approach that reminds one more of Scarlatti than of Arriaga. The final group, *Infantiles* (1937–1947), is written for piano four hands.

JESÚS GURIDI (1886–1961), of Vitoria, became one of the most important Basque composers of this century. He studied first with his mother, then with Valentín Arín in Madrid and Sáinz Basabe in Bilbao. In 1903, Guridi entered the Schola Cantorum in Paris; from there he went to Brussels and Cologne for further training. Upon returning to Bilbao, he was named professor of organ at the Academy of Music and in 1927, professor of harmony and organ at the Conservatory. In 1939, he moved to Madrid, where he devoted most of his time to composition. In 1944, he became professor of organ at the Madrid Conservatory.

Guridi is known chiefly for his *zarzuelas,* choral works, symphonic works, and studies in Basque folk music. His piano works include *Cantos populares vascos, Danzas viejas, Intermezzo,*

Lamento e imprecación de Agar (Homenaje a Arriaga), Ocho cantos, Quatorce morceaux, Vasconia, and *Tres piezas breves.*[91]

Though Antonio Fernández-Cid has found Guridi's organ works to be superior to the piano works, mention should be made of *Vasconia,* three pieces for piano on Basque folk themes.[92] Entitled "Viejo Carillon," "Leyenda," and "En el Chacoli," they show Guridi's Basque heritage coupled with some attractive, pianistic writing, though mostly of the Romantic salon variety.

JOSÉ MARÍA USANDIZAGA (1887–1915), of San Sebastián, was yet another talented Basque composer who died at a very early age (recall the great Arriaga of the early nineteenth century). After studying in San Sebastián, Usandizaga went on to Paris, where he studied piano with Francis Planté and composition with Vincent d'Indy at the Schola Cantorum. He returned to San Sebastián and became very active in the Basque musical movement, determined to create a Basque opera. After achieving local fame, he went to Madrid; one of his operas was a great success there as well as in other parts of Spain.

Usandizaga had a great melodic gift and a good flair for the theater. He showed the influence of Franck, from his training at the Schola Cantorum, and the theatrical emotionalism of Puccini. Unfortunately he died of tuberculosis at the age of 28.[93]

Compared to his works for the theater, Usandizaga's piano pieces are indeed minor compositions. They include *Trois pièces pour piano,* Op. 28; *Rapsodia vascongada; Suite para piano; Jota;* and *Chopin* (Waltz).[94]

JOSÉ MARÍA FRANCO (1894–1971), Basque violinist and composer from Irún, Guipuzcoa, began his musical studies at age six. After moving to Madrid, he entered the Madrid Conservatory, where he won prizes in piano, violin, and harmony. In 1919 he was appointed professor of violin at the Conservatory of Murcia. As a pianist, he formed part of the Quinteto Hispania, which toured Spain, South America, and Cuba. Upon returning to Spain in 1925, he was named orchestra director for Unión Radio of Madrid.

In 1927 he became a teacher of piano, organ, harmony, and composition in the Colegio Nacional de Ciegos; and in 1930 he went to Paris to present new works there. In 1932 Franco was appointed director of the Orquesta Clásica de Madrid, and in 1935 he became a professor in the vocal and instrumental division of the Madrid Conservatory. In 1939 he directed the Orquesta Filarmónica and later the Orquesta Sinfónica of Madrid.

Franco's piano works include *Miniaturas, Cantos-arca, Dos danzas españolas* (two sets), *Evocación malagueña, Tres piezas, Piezas infantiles, Escorial, Sonatina,* and *A bordo del Lucania.*

JESÚS GARCÍA LEOZ (1904–1953) was born in Olite, province of Pamplona. He began his musical training in Pamplona and later studied at the Madrid Conservatory with Conrado del Campo. He was also a student of Joaquin Turina. García Leoz was a gifted composer of film scores, song literature, and chamber music; notable in the last category is his Piano Quartet.[95] His very attractive Sonatina for piano is dedicated to his teacher Turina.

The Sonatina contains three movements. The first, in sonata–allegro design, opens with a rhythmic figure, "Spanish" in character, but soon gives way to a beautiful lyricism. The second theme proves to be one of García Leoz's most expressive statements, with attractive counterpoint in the tenor register of the piano. After a development of the opening rhythmic idea, the recapitulation begins in the tonic, F-sharp minor, but the second theme is brought back in the enharmonic key of G-flat major.

The hauntingly beautiful second movement features ostinato patterns in the lower parts against a plaintive melody in the upper part. García Leoz expands effectively to three staves in the middle of the movement to achieve the desired sonority (see Ex. 21).

The finale, the most difficult movement, is a sparkling rondo with 3/4 in the right hand against 6/8 in the left. This movement illuminates the composer's clarity of style for the piano and concludes a work that is, on the whole, above average and a very desirable piece for pianists.

Ex. 21.   García Leoz, *Sonatina*/ii/27–46. © 1945. Used by permission of the publisher, Union Musical Española.

León and Old Castile

ROGELIO VILLAR (1875–1937) was a composer/musicologist from León. He went to Madrid for further study and there worked with Llanos and Dámaso Zabalza at the Conservatory, where, in 1918, he became a professor. Villar's Romantic language is based

on the style of Grieg. The general mood is one of pastoral simplicity and elegiac melancholy, expressed with a technique that is pur-
posely naïve.[96]

In addition to the five volumes of folk songs from León with his
own harmonizations, Villar wrote *Eclogue* for orchestra, six string
quartets, songs, and piano pieces. His most typical compositions
for piano are the *Danzas montañesas,* which are built on themes
from the region of León or were inspired by their specific characteristics. As with the Romantics Chopin and Granados, Villar did
not compose them as "authentic" but as lyric, individual interpretations.[97]

VICTORIANO ECHEVARRIA (1898–1965), of Palencia, was at
one time director of the Banda Municipal Madrileña. Most of his
compositions are for orchestra, the theater, or chamber groups;
however, he did write for piano *Sonata ibérica, Ricercare,* and
Nocturno andaluz, the last an overly sentimental work.

ANTONIO-JOSÉ (1903–1936), of Burgos, wrote for piano
Danza burgalesa (a set of three), *Evocaciones, Poema de la juventud,* and *Sonata Gallega.* The sonata is a large, difficult work in
three movements that evokes the region of Galicia. According to
the score, it won a composition contest, but no details are given.

The first movement of the sonata opens in an unusual way—
"freely, in the manner of a prelude." The forceful arpeggiated
chords with modal melody "punched out" on top remind one of
César Franck's *Prelude, Chorale* and *Fugue.* The free introduction
leads into a faster section marked *Allegro apasionado,* a long,
complex sonata–allegro form.

The second movement, entitled "Cancioncilla," presents lovely
folk-song ideas. The second theme is stated more forcefully than
the first, and with thicker chords.

The third movement, a rondo, features cyclical form. The initial
rondo theme is contrasted with the introductory theme from the
first movement, the second folklike idea of movement number two,
and material from the fast section of the first movement.

The *Sonata Gallega* fluctuates between the chromaticism of

Franck and the Impressionism of Debussy, both erratically and un-evenly at times. However, the work as a whole shows a promising talent, but unfortunately Antonio-José did not live long enough to develop it properly.

Other Contemporaries

FACUNDO DE LA VIÑA (1876–1952), of Gijón, Asturias, began his studies at the Madrid Conservatory and continued them later in Paris. He became a professor at the Madrid Conservatory. Along with operas and orchestral works, he composed piano pieces including *Seis impresiones* ("Andaluza," "Culto antiguo," "La melodia," "Era el dragón . . .," "Sueños," and "La fuente abon-donada").

JOAQUÍN NIN (1879–1949), of Spanish origin, was born in Havana, Cuba. He went to Spain as a child and studied piano in Barcelona. At age fifteen he toured as a concert pianist. In 1902 he settled in Paris as a pupil of Moritz Moszkowski and of Vincent d'Indy at the Schola Cantorum. From 1908 to 1910, he lived in Berlin. Then in Havana he founded a conservatory and concert society. Nin soon returned to Europe—to Brussels and then Paris—until World War II drove him back to Havana.

Nin's edition, in two volumes, of *Classiques espagnols du piano* (1925, 1929), made available for the first time certain eighteenth- and nineteenth-century Spanish keyboard works. The importance of these two volumes, with their valuable prefaces, cannot be over-emphasized, even though Nin makes numerous emendations to the original scores.

His original works for piano include *Danse Andalouse, Danse Murcienne,* two works entitled *Danse Ibérienne, Chaîne de Valses, Message à Claude Debussy,* and *1830, Variations sur un thème frivole. Danse Murcienne* is typical of Nin's Spanish dances. Completely of the salon variety, this work alternates between "fan-tasy" sections and rhythmic/melodic elements typical of the region of Murcia.

ÁNGEL MINGOTE (1891–1961), of Daroca, Zaragoza, studied

composition in Zaragoza with Ardanús and Vega in Madrid, but he is generally considered self-taught. At age sixteen he directed a musical group in Daroca, where he eventually became organist of the basilica. Later he moved to Teruel and became pianist and conductor of the orchestra. He also became a professor of the Escuela Oficial de Jota, which is connected with the Conservatory of Zaragoza, and a professor of solfège at the Madrid Conservatory.

Mingote composed numerous works in various categories, demonstrating a solid technique. Unfortunately many of his works disappeared during the Spanish Civil War. For piano he wrote *Suite primitiva*. He was also noted for his collections of folk songs from Aragón.

MANUEL INFANTE (1883–1958) was born in Osuna, near Seville. He studied piano and composition with Morera. In 1909 Infante settled in Paris, but he did not forget the musical attractions of his native province, Andalucía.

Infante's solo piano works include *Gitanerías, Pochades Andalouses, Sevillana,* and *El Vito* (variations on a popular theme and original dance). Also popular are the *Three Andalusian Dances* ("Ritmo," "Gracia," "Sentimiento") for two pianos.

The set of variations on "El Vito," dedicated to José Iturbi, is a virtuoso salon piece in the grand manner. This attractive folk song, a *polo,* was also used for a set of variations by Joaquin Turina in the first movement of his *Sonata romántica.*[98] Infante's six variations and original Andalusian dance require a skilled performer to ferret out the theme from the difficult, but pianistic figurations. Not to be taken lightly are the treacherous left-hand leaps, seemingly so innocent at times.

MANUEL FONT Y DE ANTA (1895–1936), of Seville, began his musical training with his father and the chapelmasters Vincente Ripollés and Evaristo García Torres. Later he studied composition with Turina in Madrid and Jan Sibelius in New York. He became the director of an opera company, which took him to South America for several years. Afterwards he returned to Spain.

Besides his orchestral music, *zarzuelas,* and chamber music, Font y de Anta wrote a large, difficult suite for piano entitled *An-*

dalucía, in three volumes. Volume I contains "En el parque de María Luisa (Sevilla)," "Macarena," and "En la Alameda de Hércules"; Volume II, "La Alhambra," "El barrio de la Viña (Cádiz)," and "Perchel (Málaga)": Volume III, "En la Mezquita (Córdoba)," "En un patio sevillana," and "En los toros (Pasacalle)." Though on a grand scale and technically difficult, these "postcards" of Spain are disappointing. After one has been exposed to the descriptions given by Albéniz in *Iberia,* all others seem to fade quickly. It is interesting to note, however, that "La Alhambra" was dedicated to Arthur Rubinstein and "El barrio de la Viña" to Manuel de Falla.

JOAQUÍN NIN-CULMELL (b. 1908), son of Joaquín Nin, was born in Berlin. Nin-Culmell first studied with his father and re ceived his general education in New York and Paris, where he attended the Schola Cantorum. He studied with Dukas and later with Falla in Granada. Before retiring from teaching, he was a professor in the music department at the University of California at Berkeley.

Nin-Culmell has contributed some attractive pieces to the Spanish literature for piano—*Tres impresiones,* a sonata,[99] and a series entitled *Tonadas*. *Tres impresiones* consists of "Habanera," "Las Mozas del Cántaro," and "Un jardín de Toledo." Typical picture postcards of the salon type, they do not rank with his other works for piano.

The sonata, dedicated to Ricardo Viñes, is composed of three movements, all appealing for their clarity of style. The opening movement, an abridged sonata form, features the common interplay between 3/4 and 6/8. The many trills make for a brilliant, crisp sonority. The very brief second movement develops the rhythmic motive ♩ ♪♪ . The finale, in fast triple meter, is imitative in style with occasional inversions of the subject. By far the most difficult movement, it presents the subject in octaves near the end, making for a stirring conclusion to a well-written sonata.

The series entitled *Tonadas* represents some of the best teaching pieces in the Spanish literature from the twentieth century. Wholly pleasing to the general public, they are all based on folk material from various regions of Spain, but with modern harmonic touches.

Summary

Following the lead of Albéniz and Granados in their revival of Spanish piano music, Falla, Turina, and Mompou continued the Spanish keyboard renaissance through the first half of the twentieth century. Although Falla wrote few works for piano, his stature as a Spanish composer and the excellence of certain of these works place them among the important pieces in the literature from that period. Turina, on the other hand, wrote six times as many works for piano as did Falla. Though he often lacked the skill and inspiration of Falla, he added many colorful and nationalistic pieces to the Spanish repertoire. Mompou, that unique Catalan poet of the piano, holds a special place in the hearts of all Catalan musicians. His style essentially has not changed, either before World War II or after, as he continues to add works of exquisite beauty to the Spanish literature.

More than any other country, Spain possesses numerous folk songs/dances that have influenced composers. Since the eighteenth century, this colorful material has been the basis for countless keyboard works. On the one hand, it has resulted in scores of weak, descriptive pieces of the salon variety, what Wilfred Mellers calls "postcard music"; on the other hand, however, it has inspired some true gems for the whole of piano literature, e.g., Soler's *Fandango,* Albéniz's *Iberia,* Granados's *Goyescas,* Falla's *Cuatro piezas españolas,* Turina's *Tres danzas andaluzas,* and Mompou's *Cancion y Danza* series.

"The last refuge of poor musicians is nationalism. It is the last illusion of people without talent."[100] This very provocative pronouncement is pointed directly at composers (such as Soler, Albéniz, Granados, Falla, Turina, and Mompou) who are the musical embodiments of their country. All too often, only the negative aspects of a nationalistic composer are pointed up. One only has to examine the aforementioned works to dispel much of that negativism.

Between World War I and the 1950s, many other Spanish composers wrote piano music. Works of high standard also came from Rodolfo Halffter, before the Spanish Civil War a member of the Madrid Grupo de los Ocho; the Catalan composers Juli Garreta, Gaspar Cassadó, and Manuel Blancafort; the Valencian Manuel Palau; Oscar Esplá of the Levante; and Joaquin Nin-Culmell, who now lives in the United States. But many Spanish composers of this era continued to write descriptive, less-innovative works.

A basic trend that one finds in Spanish piano music since the eighteenth century is that of the repetition of melodic fragments, without motivic development, in order to fill out the phrases of the work. This observation parallels the conclusions of Mildred K. Ellis:

> They [the French] attach paramount importance to what they term "la première idée," "l'idée principale," or "l'inspiration mélodique," giving, perhaps, even more importance to the effectiveness of the thematic material than to its manipulation, however adroitly handled. They would reason that the effectiveness of the thematic material used by a composer in a composition depends directly upon his *sensibilité* in matters musical. This trait a composer either has or does not have, and it seems that there is nothing that can be done about it, while his skill in the manipulation of the material used as subject matter in a composition results from his musical education, which can be acquired.[101]

As with the French composers of character pieces, many Spanish keyboard composers have placed more importance on the "suggestive quality of a melody *(evocación)*" and alluring native dance rhythms than on the manipulation of material. This is a preference in compositional procedure and by no means demeans the quality of all Spanish or French works of this type. It is more a realization that one cannot compare Brahms's Sonata in F minor for solo piano with Turina's picturesque sonata *Sanlúcar de Barrameda*. They are both great works of art in their own right, but of different emphases.

CHAPTER FOUR

The Influence of the Guitar on Spanish Keyboard Music

"The natural musical feeling of the Spaniard is based on the technique of the guitar, and this has been so ever since the beginning of Spanish instrumental music."[1] Certainly no other instrument has had more influence on a nation's musical development.

There are two basic methods of playing the guitar, *rasgueado* and *punteado*. *Rasgueado* refers to repeated strummed chords. All five or six notes of the chord are seldom changed at once, and those that are retained to steady the hand produce an internal pedal point. *Punteado* refers to notes played in succession. As we shall see, the natural tuning of the open strings of the guitar (E–A–D–G–B–E) also has an influence on Spanish keyboard music.

Since the guitar was already a popular instrument in eighteenth-century Spain, it is understandable that Scarlatti should reflect some of its basic techniques in his numerous sonatas. In the words of Ralph Kirkpatrick, "As far as we know, Scarlatti never played the guitar, but surely no composer fell more deeply under its spell."[2] One of the most prominent guitar techniques used by Scarlatti is the internal pedal point. A clear example of this technique can be seen in the excerpt from Sonata K. 26/L. 368 shown in Ex. 1. Compare it with Ex. 2, taken from Albéniz's popular

"Leyenda" *(Suite Española)*. Note the wide-spaced hand-crossings in the Scarlatti and the very close finger-crossings in the Albéniz. Both contain internal pedal points. Albéniz's "Leyenda" has enjoyed popularity not only as a work for piano but also in arrangements for guitar and for marimba.

Ex. 1. Scarlatti, Sonata K. 26/L. 368/48–61. Used by permission of Belwin Mills Publishing Corp.

Ex. 2. Albéniz, "Leyenda"/1–10. Copyright © 1952 International Music Co. All rights reserved.

Passages that are strongly reminiscent of the style of the early Spanish guitar are to be found throughout Scarlatti's sonatas.

Gilbert Chase finds the most striking example to be Sonata K. 460/L. 324, "especially m. 14 onward, which is absolutely in the *punteado* style, and again from mm. 27–30, in which the combination of arpeggio chords and single detached notes, and the typical cadence, might have stemmed directly from any of the old guitar books."[3] Further evidence of guitar technique can be seen when Scarlatti builds chords by fourths (guitar tuning) instead of thirds, for example in Sonata K. 64/L. 58.

The characteristic dissonances (especially *acciaccature*) in Scarlatti's harpsichord sonatas seem to imitate the sound of the hand striking the belly of the guitar, or as Kirkpatrick puts it, "savage chords that at times almost threaten to rip the strings from the instrument."[4] A most telling illustration of this technique can be seen in Sonata K. 215/L. 323 (Ex. 3). Kirkpatrick adds that the harmonic structure of passages such as this, which imitate the guitar, seems to be determined by its open strings and by its suitability for modal Spanish folk music. To go a step further, Sonata K. 17/L. 384 may be compared with Albéniz's "El Albaicín," from *Iberia.* As Chase observes, "Both utilize the characteristic interval of the fourth in rapid 'plucked note' effects with brusque rhythmic punctuations, and with chromatic inflections peculiar to Andalusian folk music."[5] The setting is not unlike that of Falla's "Andaluza," from *Cuatro piezas españolas,* which suggests the plucked notes of a guitar at times, with pungent resounding chords accompanying a hypothetical *cante hondo* singer.[6]

Curiously enough, native Spanish composers of the eighteenth century did not show an overwhelming predilection for emulating the guitar in their keyboard works. Perhaps they considered such "gypsy music" vulgar. However, Scarlatti, a foreigner, came first to Andalusia with Maria Barbara and was, no doubt, influenced by the exotic sounds that he heard there.

Soler, Albero, Larrañaga, Blasco de Nebra, and F. Rodríguez all used guitar effects in their keyboard works, but sparingly. A powerful example of *rasgueado* technique can be seen in Blasco de Nebra's Sonata No. 3/ii (Ex. 22 in chapter 1), and a typical passage

Ex. 3. Scarlatti, Sonata K. 215/L. 323/42–51. © 1953 G. Schirmer, Inc.
Used by permission.

with internal pedal point in F. Rodríguez's Sonata in F minor/i (Ex.
26 in chapter 1).

In the early nineteenth century in Spain Italian opera reigned
supreme, and Spanish composers of piano music contributed only
light salon music and fantasies on operatic themes or continued the
style galant. Naturally, guitar techniques were not generally
needed in this setting. However, with Albéniz, Granados, Falla,
and Turina, in the late nineteenth and early twentieth centuries,
there was a revival of Spanish keyboard music. Guitar effects
permeate the piano works of these composers and reflect the
Spanish nationalistic spirit.

Guitar effects abound in the piano music of Turina.[7] Examples of
sonorities based on the tuning of the guitar can be found in
"Zambra," from *Cinco danzas gitanas,* Op. 55; "Zarabanda," from
the *Partita en do,* Op. 57; and "La mocita del barrio," from
Mujeres de Sevilla, Op. 89. These inherently quartal structures are
used in strikingly different ways in these pieces. The approach in
"Zambra" is strong, rhythmic, and percussive, employing a combination of the *rasgueado* and *punteado* techniques (Ex. 4). In "La
mocita del barrio" the chords, which reproduce the open strings of
the guitar exactly (E–A–D–G–B–E), help create a lyrical, languid
atmosphere (Ex. 5).

Ex. 4. Turina, "Zambra"/9–13. © 1930 Editions Salabert. Used by permission.

Ex. 5. Turina, "La mocita del barrio"/1–4. © 1935 Lerolle. Used by permission.

The technique of fast repeated chords on the guitar is relatively simple compared with the same technique on the piano. On the guitar, it is a matter of strumming the hand down *and* up, the sonority being achieved with both strokes. On the piano, the sound occurs only on the downward movement, so that the hand must be lifted constantly. If one is not careful, this action can result in semi-paralysis, or a "clutched" feeling, preventing the performer from articulating the passage clearly. Thus, what is comparatively simple on the guitar becomes difficult when transferred to the piano. Turina's "Generalife," from *Cinco danzas gitanas,* Op. 55, affords an example of this pianistic problem (see Ex. 6).

Ex. 6. Turina, "Generalife"/77–83. © 1930 Editions Salabert. Used by permission.

Turina makes *specific* reference to the guitar in only two works for piano, Prelude No. 4 (from *Preludios,* Op. 80) and *Rincón mágico,* Op. 97. In the former he indicates *como una guitarra* beneath a rhythmically accented bass line. One immediately thinks of the brilliant, strong thumb technique *(pulgado)* used by many flamenco guitarists for lower lines of this type (see Ex. 7). In a similar case, Debussy indicates a guitar-like effect by writing "quasi guitarra" at the beginning of his prelude *La sérénade interrompue.* Granados also was interested in emulating the low, rich tones of the guitar in his "Coloquio en la reja," from *Goyescas.* A footnote at the opening of this work reads, "Toutes les basses imitant la guitare." In the first movement of Turina's descriptive sonata *Rincón mágico,* Op. 97, a theme and variations, the composer asks for a guitar effect by entitling Variation I "Regino y la guitarra." Amidst typical guitar rhythms and chords, Turina employs the exact intervals of guitar tuning in arpeggios. In a similar way, Granados ends *Goyescas* with an arpeggiated sonority based on the open strings of the guitar (see Ex. 8).

Ex. 7.   Turina, Prelude No. 4/9–12. © 1934. Used by permission of the publisher, Union Musical Española.

Two striking examples of the brusque, savage use of *rasgueado* and *punteado* effects in Spanish piano music can be seen in Albéniz's "El Puerto," from *Iberia* (Ex. 9) and Falla's "Andaluza," from *Cuatro piezas españolas* (Ex. 2 in chapter 3). The intentions of the composers are extremely clear. Albéniz marks his passage *rudement marqué et bien sec* and Falla marks his *très rhythmé et avec un sentiment sauvage.* Both examples are replete

Ex. 8.   Granados, *Epilogo* "Serenata del Espectro" /246–262. © 1972. Used by permission of the publisher, Union Musical Española.

Ex. 9.   Albéniz, "El Puerto"/41–48. Used by permission of Belwin Mills Publishing Corp.

with accent marks and dynamics of *fortissimo*. By his telling use of dissonance, Falla enhances the effect of his work with chords that almost sound metallic. But Falla seems to go a step further in his *Fantasía bética* (Ex. 5 in chapter 3), where he combines guitar effects with even more modern tendencies. In the words of John

Trend, it "possibly represents the farthest that Falla has gone in adapting the harmonic peculiarities of the guitar to the modern pianoforte."[8] Trend also adds that Falla's *Fantasía bética* makes an interesting comparison with his *Homenaje* in memory of Debussy, which was originally written for guitar and then arranged for piano by the composer.

Thus, the spirit of the guitar and its effects play a vital role in Spanish piano music and its technique. Pianists, especially those who are not Spanish, should constantly remember that at the back of many Spanish composers' minds there is often a plucked instrument, the guitar, the chords of which sometimes give the effect of an appoggiatura and add a vital pulse to the rhythm. This wedding of the two instruments has been described by Joaquin Rodrigo in a most unusual way. He describes the ideal guitar dreamt of by Spanish composers as "a strange, fantastic, multiform instrument which has the wings of the harp, the tail of the piano, and the soul of a guitar."[9]

Though some Spanish composers of piano music after Manuel de Falla have been influenced by the guitar and its techniques, the more progressive ones have chosen to steer clear of sonorities that immediately remind one of folk elements. The more recent composers generally prefer a trend toward universalization; consequently the guitar has not figured as prominently in the music of Spain since World War II.

CHAPTER FIVE

Spanish Piano Music since World War II

Introduction

The Spanish Civil War (1936–1939) dealt a cultural blow to Spain, as did World War II to the whole of Europe. By the end of the civil strife in Spain, many of the nation's most important composers and performers had left their native land and musical life had come to a virtual standstill. In 1949 some composers in Barcelona made the first attempt to revive Spanish musical activities and to bring musical composition in Spain more into line with what was and had been happening elsewhere in the world. This group, calling itself the Manuel de Falla Circle, was influenced by the works of Bartók, Stravinsky, Hindemith, and the Viennese school. The members of the Circle were Juan Comellas, Alberto Blancafort, Manuel Valls, Ángel Cerdá, Josep Cercós, and Josep Mestres Quadreny. Their activities, which continued until 1955, were sponsored by the French Institute and Club 49, a group of private patrons in Barcelona. Another important event for Barcelona was the first concert of new music (Boulez, Nono, Stockhausen) in postwar Spain, presented in 1955. By 1959, a more avante-garde group, Música Abierta, had been formed in Barcelona by Juan Hidalgo, Josep Cercós, Josep Mestres Quadreny, Joaquim Homs, and Luis de Pablo.

Though Barcelona made the first strides in "modernizing" Spain's music after the war, Madrid was not far behind. In 1958 the Grupo Nueva Música was formed in Madrid. The membership included Ramón Barce, Cristóbal Halffter, Antón García-Abril, Luis de Pablo, Fernando Ember, Manuel Moreno Buendía, Enrique Franco, and Manuel Carra. In 1965 the Alea Electronic Studio was founded in Madrid by Luis de Pablo.

In the nineteenth century and the first half of the twentieth, most Spanish composers sought musical training in Paris. Since World War II, studies of new techniques have been centered in Italy and Germany, especially at the summer courses in Darmstadt.

Though since the 1950s many Spanish musicians have been trying to break away from writing nationalistic music, Tomás Marco contends that Spanish composers have rarely been able to write completely from a point of abstraction. He claims that the "Spanishness" of their creative personalities is bound to come out in some fashion and finds the following Spanish characteristics in some twentieth-century works: (1) a direct expressive quality that intentionally avoids over-elaborate techniques of composition, (2) a certain quality of violence or forcibleness, and (3) particular spatial-temporal relationships that include a highly individualistic conception of rhythm, incessantly repeated elaboration of certain materials, and remarkable handling of the aleatory factor.[1] Though a case could be made for items (1), (2), and part of (3), it seems difficult to envision a "Spanish" way of handling aleatory procedures.

Many of the contemporaries of Manuel de Falla have continued to write piano works since World War II, but most have not experimented with the new techniques ushered in during the 1950s. This chapter will concern itself mainly with the new generations and the new trends in piano music adopted by Spanish composers from outside influences. One only has to examine a few piano scores published by Editorial de Música Española Contemporánea (Madrid and Barcelona) to see that Spanish composers are incorporating the latest techniques in writing for piano.

Barcelona: The Manuel de Falla Circle

JUAN COMELLAS (b. 1913), of Barcelona, was self-taught, for the most part, in composition. He has produced numerous works for orchestra, for the theater, for chamber and choral groups, and for voice and piano, as well as a substantial contribution to the literature for piano. His piano works consist of *Homenaje a Ravel, Tonadas infantiles, Homenaje a Falla,* two Sonatinas, *Las sonatas de París,* a Sonata, *Homenaje a Mompou, Nanas, Les voltes, Tres andorranas,* and *Los acordes de verano.*

ALBERTO BLANCAFORT (b. 1928), of La Garriga, Barcelona, studied in Paris with Olivier Messiaen, René Leibowitz, and Nadia Boulanger. Besides his excellent Sonata for piano, he has written numerous film scores.

The Sonata contains three contrasting movements. The first, in sonata form, opens with a narrow-range melody, hauntingly lyric, accompanied by a difficult undulating pattern. Though contrasting ideas are presented, this material provides the most interest. The second movement is in ternary form, the first and last sections being basically chordal, but graced with beautiful ornamentation in the Spanish style. The middle section features a plaintive melody in the treble set off by a walking *basso ostinato,* an effective contrast to the first and final sections of the movement. The finale proves to be of the *perpetuum mobile* variety, marked *prestissimo,* and presents a constant swirl of sound from beginning to end.

MANUEL VALLS GORINA (b. 1920), of Badalona, Barcelona, studied at the Conservatorio del Liceo and the University of Barcelona. He was one of the founders of the Manuel de Falla Circle. Valls describes his style as "free atonalism" in which the influence of Bartók, Roussel, and Stravinsky can be heard.[2] Though today he is known mostly as a writer on music, Valls has composed for piano *Tres preludios, Suite (homenaje a Falla),* Sonata, *Tocata,* and *Preludio alegre.*

ÁNGEL CERDÁ (b. 1924), of Oviedo, has written three sonatas

for piano and, according to Manuel Valls, the first two represent some of the best modern works from Catalonia in that genre.[3]

JOSEP CERCÓS (b. 1925), of Barcelona, began writing in a style influenced by German Romanticism, but soon moved on to a style reminiscent of Webern and Henze, passing through Wolf, Mahler, Schönberg, and Hindemith. Though introduced to the twelve-tone method by Hermann Scherchen, Cercós has shown a preference for synthetic scales instead of a specific compositional system such as a serial technique.[4]

For keyboard, Cercós has written two Sonatas for harpsichord and *Preludios ambulantes* and Sonata for piano. The piano Sonata in four movements shows an angular, rugged, dissonant style that often smacks of Hindemith. The first movement is a long, complex sonata form. The second is marked *prestissimo* and features fast, repeated chords for the accompaniment. The third movement, *Tempo de Forlana*, displays the characteristic dotted patterns in 6/8 commonly associated with this dance form. The movement concludes with a cadenza section that leads into the finale, a rondo. Cercós's pianistic style is difficult, often unidiomatic to the instrument and at times austere.

JOSEP MESTRES QUADRENY (b. 1929), of Manresa, studied at the University of Barcelona, but is self-taught in contemporary techniques. He has worked in the Electronic Music Laboratory of Barcelona since it was established in 1968. His serial technique, which he started in 1957, evolved toward procedures of continuous variation based on interval–duration relationships. In 1960, Mestres Quadreny began experimenting with chance elements in his music, and since 1965 has been incorporating electronic processes in some works.[5] His piano works are early compositions, including *Tocata, Suite en do,* and Sonata, a serial work written in 1958.

Others Associated with Barcelona

JOAQUIM HOMS (b. 1906), of Barcelona, has been an industrial engineer as well as composer. Though mostly self-taught in piano and composition, he studied composition with Roberto Gerhard from 1930 to 1936. In 1959 he joined the group called Musica Abierta, which introduced avant-garde works of North America to Barcelona.

Homs's piano works consist of a series of *Impromptus*, numbers 6 and 7 (1960) employing the serial technique. Though he was familiar with the works of Webern as early as 1936, he did not adopt the twelve-tone method until 1953.[6]

XAVIER MONTSALVATGE (b. 1912), of Gerona, studied at the Barcelona Municipal Conservatory with Enric Morera and Jaime Pahissa. He has taught in Barcelona at the San Jorge Academy of Fine Arts, the Destino Seminary, and, more recently, at the Municipal Conservatory. He has also been an editor and music critic for the Barcelona newspaper *La vanguardia* since 1962. In 1970 Montsalvatge became president of the advisory council of the music commission of the General Directorate of Fine Arts.[7]

Montsalvatge was primarily self-taught as a composer, his music being influenced in the beginning by Stravinsky, Bartók, and the post-Impressionistic French composers. His early works were nationalistic, yielding to polytonal, twelve-tone, and post-serial methods.[8] The piano works do not form a major genre in his total output, but certainly merit discussion. They include *Tres impromptus*, *Tres divertimentos*, *Ritmos*, *Bourée*, *Divagación*, *Sketch*, and *Sonatine pour Yvette*.

Sketch, a *habanera*, was one of Montsalvatge's earliest works, forming part of a ballet written in 1936. Later it was used as part of the symphonic suite *Calidoscopio*, and in 1944 it was transcribed for violin and piano and retitled *A la moda de 1912*. Further revisions were made in 1968, resulting in the version for solo piano. *Divagación* also underwent a change. Originally it was an interlude in the opera *El gato con botas*.

The *Three Divertissements (On Themes of Forgotten Composers)* have an air of the Stravinskian burlesque style, according to Manuel Valls.[9] Through a friend, Montsalvatge became familiar with these dance melodies, which supposedly enjoyed popularity at village feasts. The three works represent the *schottische*, the *habanera,* and the waltz (with the flair of the *jota*), respectively. They all show Montsalvatge's skilled use of polytonality, and the *habanera* displays a careful awareness of voice leading. These dances can be considered Montsalvatge's opus one, since they appeared in 1941, the year that he considered himself an independent composer.

Montsalvatge's largest work for piano is *Sonatine pour Yvette,* in three movements. According to the composer, he wrote it as agile and youthful music, reminiscent of his daughter.[10] Of course, the work is not what one would call "music for children." The first movement abounds with spirit and lightness, displaying rippling 6/8 patterns and a fliud chromaticism that is 'very logically worked out. The second movement, more serious, is unified by a series of chord clusters with a repeated rhythmic pattern. The finale, a flashy toccata movement, uses a popular children's tune for its main thematic material. Ex. 1 shows the theme in a virtuosic figuration near the conclusion of the work.

Ex. 1. Montsalvatge, *Sonatine pour Yvette*/iii/81–88. © 1962 Editions Salabert. Used by permission.

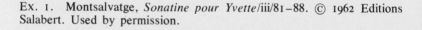

JUAN HIDALGO (b. 1927), of Las Palmas, Canary Islands, studied at the Marshall Academy in Barcelona with Montsalvatge and later with Boulanger. He continued his studies with Bruno

Maderna in Milan and participated in the activities at Darmstadt in 1957. In 1958, he returned to Darmstadt, where he met John Cage, who had a great influence on his style. In 1960, Hidalgo, along with Walter Marchetti, organized the contemporary music society Música Abierta for the Club 49 in Barcelona. Since 1973, Hidalgo has lived in Milan.

Hidalgo has contributed several avant-garde works for piano, including *A Letter for David Tudor,* for a pianist, piano, and as many objects as are necessary; a series of four works entitled *Armandia,* involving from three to eight pianists; *Aulaga; Milan Piano,* for one pianist, grand piano, and any kind of instruments or objects with which one can produce undetermined sounds; *Tamaran,* for an undetermined number of pianos; and *Wuppertal Dos Pianos,* for two pianos.

XAVIER BENGUEREL (b. 1931), a native of Barcelona, lived for some time in Santiago, Chile, where he began his musical studies. He returned to Spain in 1954. For the most part he is self-taught, but has been influenced by the Impressionists, Bartók, Schönberg, and Webern. In the mid-1950s he embraced serialism.[11]

Benguerel's *Suite* for piano shows expert handling, in a twentieth-century manner, of the Baroque suite. This modern set of dances consists of Preludio, Corrente, Sarabanda, Gavotta, Musette, Badinerie, and Giga. The Gavotta and complementary Musette especially are in the Bach style, with a typically restricted register for the accompaniment in the Musette. Benguerel has also written a Sonata for piano.

JOAN GUINJOAN (b. 1931), of Riudoms, Tarragona, studied at at the Conservatory of the Liceo in Barcelona and at the l'Ecole Normale de Musique in Paris. Between 1958 and 1960 he supposedly gave more than two hundred piano recitals in Spain, France, and Germany. He has won numerous prizes in music, participated in several seminars on music, and written many articles. His compositions are beginning to capture the attention of audiences in Europe and America.

Guinjoan's works for piano include *Tres pequeñas piezas,*

Scherzo y Trio, three *Preludios, El pinell de dalt, Momentos No. 1, Digraf, Fantasia en do, Chez Garcia Ramos, Celulas No. 1,* and *Celulas No. 3 (Celulas No. 2* is for celesta, marimba, and piano). *Celulas No. 1* (1967) belongs to the composer's twelve-tone period. The title comes from the structure of the material composed by segmented series, superimposed and related by means of diverse combinatorial methods that establish a pointillistic style.

JAIME PADRÓS MONTORIOL (b. 1926), of Igualada, Barcelona, has contributed *Preludio y danza,* Sonata, *Estudio y Sardana,* and *Zapateado* to the Spanish piano literature.

NARCISO BONET (b. 1933), of Barcelona, began his musical training in his native Catalan city, but soon went to Paris to work with Boulanger. He returned to Barcelona in 1955 to become very active in the musical life of that city. His piano works include *Cinco nocturnos, Octaedre,* and Sonata.

JORDI CERVELLO (b. 1935), of Barcelona, began studying the violin at age six. Later he studied in Milan at the Verdi Conservatory. Though he leans more toward string music, he has written an homage to Arthur Rubinstein for piano entitled *Balada.*

JOSEP SOLER (b. 1935) has written *Tres peçes per a piano,* three difficult works that cover the gamut of the keyboard using modern techniques associated with the post-Webern era.

Madrid: The Grupo Nueva Música

RAMÓN BARCE (b. 1928), of Madrid, studied at the Madrid Conservatory and at the University of Madrid, where he earned a Ph.D. in linguistics. In 1958, together with other young composers, he founded the group Nueva Música. Since 1967 he has directed the Sonda concerts and the magazine of the same name, which is dedicated exclusively to contemporary music. Barce has written numerous articles and edited a Spanish version of Schönberg's *Style and Idea* and *Treatise on Harmony.*

Taking Schönberg as a point of departure, Barce began composing in an atonal style quite early. A collection of piano pieces entitled *Estudios seriales* demonstrates Barce's "extreme van-guardism," to use the composer's own term.[12] Regarding *Estudio de sonoridades,* from the above set, the composer says: "I intended, for some years, to create new forms for each work. . . . In *Estudio de sonoridades,* for piano, I employed a counterpoint of dynamics, registers, and sonorities."[13] Arthur Custer states that this work "is concerned almost exclusively with timbre. A rhythmic cell serves as the foundation for the entire work, and its manipulation employs all types of effects typical of virtuoso piano writing since World War II."[14]

The set also includes *Estudio de impulsos, Estudio de valores,* and *Estudio de densidades.* In the last piece, each section employs ten or eleven notes and excludes the remaining note or notes of the chromatic scale. Then follows a passage saturated with the missing notes. Thus the work is played with the absence or predominance of certain notes.

Barce has also written *Homenaje a Reger, Nueve pequeñas preludios,* and sixteen *Preludios* for piano.

CRISTÓBAL HALFFTER (b. 1930), of Madrid, nephew of Ernesto and Rodolfo Halffter, studied composition with Conrado del Campo at the Madrid Conservatory. He also studied privately with Alexander Tansman. From 1955 to 1963, C. Halffter conducted the Orchestra Manuel de Falla; from 1965 to 1966, he was music director of the Madrid Radio Symphony Orchestra; and from 1962 to 1966, he taught at the Madrid Conservatory, becoming its director in 1964. His works have received international recognition, and he stands as one of Spain's most important composers since World War II.

For the piano, C. Halffter has written a Sonata and *Introduccion, fuga y final,* Op. 15. The early Sonata is a well-constructed Neo-classic work that deserves more attention by pianists. In the development section it is reminiscent of the style of Rodolfo Halffter's *Dos sonatas de El Escorial* but it is more extended than either of them. C. Halffter's Sonata is typically Spanish, with its interplay between 6/8 and 3/4.

C. Halffter was attracted to the music of Ernesto Halffter because of its "original treatment of Spanish folklore," but it was the "decisive influence" of Rodolfo Halffter's polytonality that led him ultimately to write atonally.[15] In 1956, C. Halffter began writing serial pieces. His first twelve-tone work was *Tres piezas* for string quartet, Op. 9. Later came his important serial work for piano, *Introduccion, fuga y final*, Op. 15. He once stated that his greatest aspiration was to "Latinize serialism."[16]

Introduccion, fuga y final is based on the following tone row: E-flat–G–C-sharp–D–F–C–B–E–F-sharp–G-sharp–A–B-flat. Ex. 2 shows the conclusion of the Introduction and the beginning of the Fugue (m. 30, *Allegro Molto Moderato*). The fugue subject presents the original form of the row while the answer presents it transposed to start on B-flat, in the traditional tonic–dominant relationship. An unusual aspect of this twelve-tone fugue is Halffter's use of the head motif in its original form as well as inverted. This procedure plays an important part in the entire section.

It should also be mentioned that C. Halffter has written an aleatory work, *Formantes*, Op 26, for two pianos.

ANTON GARCÍA ABRIL (b. 1933), of Teruel, studied composition with Manuel Palau at the Valencia Conservatory and with Julio Gómez at the Madrid Conservatory. He also did work at the Accadèmia Chigiana in Siena, Italy, and the Accadèmia di S. Cecilia in Rome. García Abril has taught at the Madrid Conservatory since 1957 and has composed numerous scores for theater, film, and television.

He has written a concerto for piano and orchestra, *Danzas concertantes* for piano and orchestra, a piano quartet, and a very attractive Sonatina for solo piano. The Sonatina is in three movements—Allegretto, Arieta, Finale—and is wholly pianistic and quite satisfying in its entirety. A Neoclassic work, it is clear, fluid, and readily appealing. The first movement contains a most effective main theme in a modal style. The second movement features widely spaced sonorities and lends itself to telling voicing of counter-melodies in the tenor register of the piano. The finale is a vivacious rondo with a time signature of 3/4 6/8.

Ex. 2.   C. Halffter, *Introduccion, fuga y final*/27–37. © 1959. Used by permission of the publisher, Union Musical Española.

LUIS DE PABLO is one of Spain's most important figures associated with modern music. He was born in 1930 in Bilbao, and studied law at the University of Madrid and music at the Madrid Conservatory. He attended the summer courses at Darmstadt and was greatly influenced by Olivier Messiaen, Karlheinz Stockhausen, Pierre Boulez, and György Ligeti. Pablo founded the performance groups Tiempo y Música (1959) and Alea Electronic Studio (1965), directed the Juventudes Musicales in 1960, and was responsible for arranging the first Biennial of New Music, in Madrid in 1964.

His early works were influenced by Falla and Bartók, but he later withdrew them and labeled his first twelve-tone piece, *Coral* for woodwinds, his opus one. During the period 1953–1959, the Boulez circle had the most influence on his style.[17] Pablo's piano works consist of *Gárgolas, Sonatina giocosa, Libro para el pianista,* and Sonata, Op. 3. *Movil I,* for two pianos, shows Pablo's experiments with aleatory procedures; and *Progressus,* Op. 8, also for two pianos, is based on two series, one forming the linear direction of the piece, the other controlling the dynamics.

The well-constructed Sonata, Op. 3, a twelve-tone work, is in one movement but is divided into four contrasting sections, giving the effect of separate movements. Pablo labels them *Invención rítmica libre, Canon, Grupos verticales,* and *Final.* All sections employ only the original series and its inversion.

The row consists of the pitches E–G–D-sharp–D–G-flat– A–B-flat–B–D-flat–C–F–A-flat. Ex. 3 shows the tone row from the opening of the sonata; Ex. 4 illustrates the canon (inverted); Ex. 5 shows the row material used as "vertical groups"; and Ex. 6 illustrates Pablo's expert weaving of the two versions of the row, with dynamics playing an all-important part in singling out the original form of the series.

Ex. 3. Pablo, Sonata, Op. 3/1–2. © 1960. Used by permission of the publisher, Union Musical Española.

Ex. 4. Pablo, Sonata, Op. 3/49–53. © 1960. Used by permission of the publisher, Union Musical Española.

Ex. 5. Pablo, Sonata, Op. 3/109–115. © 1960. Used by permission of the publisher. Union Musical Española.

Ex. 6. Pablo, Sonata, Op. 3/148–152. © 1960. Used by permission of the publisher, Union Musical Española.

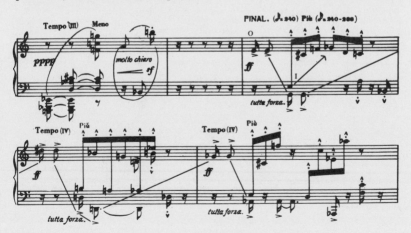

Similar to Stockhausen's *Klavierstück XI,* Pablo's *Libro para el pianista* gives the performer "sonorous objects," the ordering of which is largely a matter of free choice. For example, the third movement is played from a twelve-page manuscript in which the staves are divided by a narrow wooden ridge, making it possible for the performer to play the top staff of page 1 with the bottom staff of page 3, or any of the 254 possible combinations.[18]

MANUEL CARRA (b. 1931), of Málaga, studied at the conservatory in his native city, then went to Madrid to study piano with José Cubiles. Today Carra is one of Spain's noted pianists. *Transformaciones sobre una estructura de Cristóbal Halffter* for two pianos and *Cuatro piezas breves* for solo piano are two of his major works. Arthur Custer finds that the *Cuatro piezas breves*

> show a remarkable cohesiveness and exhibit skilled treatment of the climax in each movement. In the first piece, the climax is represented, a little more than halfway through, by a carefully prepared twelve-tone *fortissimo* chord, while in the second it is achieved by means of a single accented note. In the third movement, the climax occurs early, in a three-note *fortissimo* chord that spans six octaves, and in the fourth, a series of closely spaced accented notes leaps out of the figuration, creating a climax that is at once dynamic and linear.[19]

Especially interesting is the second piece, based on a twelve-tone figure that is palindromic with respect to rhythm, dynamics, and texture (see Ex. 7).

Ex. 7.   Carra, *Cuatro piezas breves*/No. 2/1–8. © 1960. Used by permission of the publisher, Union Musical Española.

MANUEL MORENO BUENDÍA (b. 1932), of Murcia, has written Sonata and *Suite miniatura* for piano.

Others Associated with Madrid

Unlike his brother Rodolfo, ERNESTO HALFFTER (b. 1905) has changed his piano style little since World War II. A fairly recent work for piano, *Preludio y Danza* (1974), retains the sterner, more severe style in the Prelude, and is reminiscent of his *Llanto por Ricardo Viñes* (1940). However, the Dance has a mixture of elements, some typically Spanish passages with Phrygian overtones, some Prokofievian wit, and even some Impressionistic harmonies at times. Both movements have tonal foundations, regardless of the level of dissonance achieved.

FRANCISCO ESCUDERO (b. 1913), of San Sebastián, studied at the conservatory of his native Basque city. Later he continued his musical studies with Conrado del Campo in Madrid and Paul Dukas in Paris. He has written Sonata, *Veinticuatro piezas breves,* and *Dos fugas* for piano.

MIGUEL ASINS ARBÓ (b. 1916), though a native of Barcelona, has not contributed actively to modern Catalan music. He studied with Manuel Palau at the Conservatory of Valencia and worked for a few years in Madrid. His compositions for piano consist of *Cuatro melodías populares castellanas, Tres danzas españolas, Dansa catalana, Suite ampurdanesa, Canción (homenaje a Albéniz),* and *Flamenco.*

FRANCISCO CALÉS OTERO (b. 1925), of Madrid, has composed Sonata, *Scherzo-fantasía,* and *Divertimento* for piano.

AUGUSTÍN GONZÁLEZ ACILU (b. 1925), of Alsasua, Navarra, began his musical studies in his native city, then continued at the Madrid Conservatory. He has also done studies in musicology related to the Navarra region. As have many of his colleagues, he has attended courses in new music at Darmstadt. Gonzáles Acilu has written *Presencias, Rasgos,* and *Tres movimientos* for piano and *Pulsiones* for harpsichord. A product of his stay in Paris, *Tres movimientos* represents one of his first serial works.

CARMELO ALONSO BERNAOLA (b. 1929), of Ochandiano, Vizcaya, studied with Francisco Calés and Julio Gómez at the Madrid Conservatory as well as with Goffredo Petrassi in Rome. He also attended sessions at Darmstadt. Though he has written serial works and experimented with newer techniques, his piano work *Tres aires castellanos* belongs to his early period of composition. A work using more modern trends is *Morfologia sonora,* written for Pedro Espinosa (b. 1934), one of Spain's most important interpreters of contemporary piano music.

CLAUDIO PRIETO (b. 1934), of Muñeca de la Peña, Palencia, studied in El Escorial, Madrid, and Rome, to include work with Bruno Maderna and Goffredo Petrassi. The list of awards and prizes to his credit is quite lengthy. Among his compositions can be found an avant-garde work for piano entitled *Juguetes para pianistas.*

GONZALO DE OLAVIDE (b. 1934), of Madrid, studied composition and piano in the conservatories of Brussels and Antwerp.

From 1960 to 1964 he participated in courses at Darmstadt, under the direction of Pierre Boulez and Luciano Berio. At present, he lives in Geneva. Olavide has done much work in the field of electronic music. A recent work for piano is the *Sonata della Ricordanza*.

ÁNGEL OLIVER (b. 1937), of Moyuela, Zaragoza, began his musical training with his father and eventually went on to study at the Madrid Conservatory. His teachers included Cristóbal Halffter and Jesús Guridi. Oliver also studied in Rome at the Academy of St. Cecilia and later took courses at Darmstadt. He has numerous awards to his credit. Since 1965 he has been a professor at the Madrid Conservatory and the Escuelas Universitarias del Profesorado. His piano scores include *Invenciones* and *Psicograma No. 1* (No. 2 is for guitar and No. 3 is for violin, viola, cello, and piano).

MIGUEL ÁNGEL CORIA (b. 1937), of Madrid, attended the Madrid Conservatory and from 1966 to 1967 studied at the electronic studio of the University of Utrecht. In 1964, with Luis de Pablo, he founded the Alea Electronic Studio. For piano, Coria has written *Juego de densidades, En rouge et noir* (actually twelve proposals for any instrument), and *Dos piezas para piano*.

The brief *Dos piezas* consist of "Ravel for President" and "Frase." The first piece presents Impressionistic devices such as harmonic planing and tremulando effects, but concludes with the lyrical Ravel-like melody accompanied by cluster chords. In order to shape the second piece, the composer has made use of musical "kitsch," with indications such as *Ardente d'amore* and *agitato,* along with the air of a waltz.

JESÚS VILLA ROJO (b. 1940), of Brihuega, studied clarinet, piano, violin, and composition at the Madrid Conservatory. He also studied electronic music in Rome at the Academy of St. Cecilia. He was the founder of the Forum Players in Rome and is the artistic director of LIM (Laboratory of Musical Interpretation) in Madrid. For the piano, Villa Rojo has composed *Neuve piezas breves*.

FRANCISCO CANO (b. 1940), of Madrid, studied at the conservatory there, having been a student of Cristóbal Halffter, Francisco Calés, and Gerardo Gombau. Cano was the recipient of a scholarship from the Ministerio de Educación y Ciencia and from the Juan March Foundation. One of his recent works for piano is entitled *Continuo*.

CARLOS CRUZ DE CASTRO (b. 1941), of Madrid, studied at the Madrid Conservatory as well as the Hochschule Robert Schumann in Düsseldorf. He has worked in two electronic studios, the Alea in Madrid and the Robert Schumann Laboratory in Düsseldorf. Cruz de Castro's piano works include *Domino-Klavier* (for any keyboard instrument) and *Llámalo como quieras,* a large score. The preface to the latter work contains performance instructions for the various symbols employed. Ex. 8 shows the opening page from this unusual work. The score has indications for vocal sounds, the snapping of fingers, a stroke on the leg, and the clapping of hands, in addition to the standard notation. The metronome continues throughout the work.

Ex. 8.   Cruz de Castro, *Llámalo como quieras*/opening page. © 1974 Carlos Cruz de Castro. Used by permission of Editorial de Música Española Contemporánea.

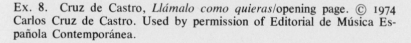

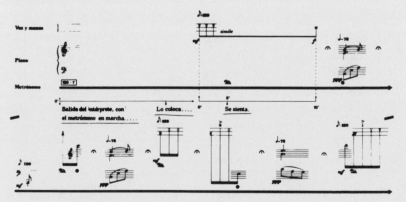

TOMÁS MARCO (b. 1942), of Madrid, has studied law, psychology, sociology, and Germanic philology in addition to music.

In the area of composition, he has worked with such notables as Pierre Boulez, Karlheinz Stockhausen, Bruno Maderna, and György Ligeti and has published important works on modern music. From 1973 to 1976 he was professor of music history at Universidad Nacional de Educación a Distancia and since 1973 has been professor of new techniques at the Madrid Conservatory. His music has begun to attract international attention.

Marco's works for piano include *Temporalia* and *Fetiches*. The title of the latter refers to certain fetishistic elements in the music at the moment of its composition. The intervals employed are expanded parallel to the changes of register, moving from simple events, through a brilliant passage in octaves, to clusters at the conclusion. The piece consists of 41 segments of music separated by three different classes of pauses—short, mid-length, or long. Though the work is subject to various interpretations in certain passages, it is by no means a chance piece, as is Stockhausen's *Klavierstücke XI*.

Seville and Other Regions

MANUEL CASTILLO (b. 1930), originally of Seville, studied first in his native city then went on to work with Lucas Moreno and Conrado del Campo in Madrid. From Madrid, he went to Paris for further study with Nadia Boulanger. He became a member of the piano faculty at the Conservatory of Seville in 1956 and its director in 1964.

In 1959 Castillo won Spain's National Prize in music for his *Preludio, Diferencias y Toccata (sobre un tema de Isaac Albéniz)*, in honor of the famed composer who wrote so many Andalusian works. Other piano compositions by Castillo include *Tiempo de danza, Andaluza, Apuntes de Navidad, Allegro, Suite Nocturnos, Preludio para la mano izquierda, Tres impresiones*, Sonata, Sonatina, and *Tocata*.

The *Preludio, Diferencias y Toccata* is an exceptional work based on the main theme from Albéniz's "El Puerto" (*Iberia*, Book I). The source of the thematic material is not readily apparent in the *Preludio,* which uses only a motive from the original tune. However, Castillo produces the borrowed theme at the opening of the *Diferencias* and takes it through a myriad of pitch and rhythmic transformations. The *Toccata* emphasizes the "hammering," repetitive aspect of the theme, giving the finale a motoristic quality.

MATILDE SALVADOR (b. 1918), of Castellón, is one of the few women composers from Spain. She regarded her husband, the Valencian composer Vicente Asencio, as her mentor in piano and composition. Salvador is mostly known for her vocal music, but she has written a Sonatina and *Planyivola* for piano.

MANUEL ANGULO (b. 1930), of Campo de Criptana, Ciudad Real, has written a *Suite* for piano.

Two Spanish Composers of North America

RODOLFO HALFFTER (b. 1900), a citizen of Mexico since 1940, began composing with the twelve-tone technique in 1953; *Tres hojas de album,* Op. 22, is his first serial work for piano. Others that followed include *Música para dos pianos,* Op. 29; *Tercera Sonata,* Op. 30; *Laberinto,* Op. 34; and *Nocturno,* Op. 36. Halffter states that his serial works are the result of a slow evolution and that they are really very similar to his earlier, polytonal works.[20]

R. Halffter's third Sonata, Op. 30, is a tightly knit work in four movements based on the same tone row: D–E–B-flat–F-sharp–A–F–G–C-sharp–D-sharp–C–G-sharp–B. In this sonata Halffter updates his basic style since World War II and employs some unusual symbols: e.g., indications for long notes of undetermined duration, for pressing down notes without their sounding (a technique that dates back to Henry Cowell), and for repeating a pattern a certain number of seconds. *Laberinto* ("Labyrinth"), Op. 34, employs similiar new techniques. It has the amusing subtitle *Cuatro intentos de acertar con la salida* ("Four Attempts to Locate the Exit"). All four movements are entitled *Intento,* and all conclude with the note F in the treble and bass, spaced six octaves apart.

This sameness gives the work a certain unity but causes one to wonder if the exit was indeed found.

CARLOS SURIÑACH (b. 1915), of Barcelona, studied at the Barcelona Municipal Conservatory, the Robert Schumann Conservatory in Düsseldorf, the Cologne Hochschule für Musik, and the Prussian Academy of the Arts in Berlin. He was conductor of the Barcelona Philharmonic Orchestra, 1944–1947, and the Gran Teatro del Liceo opera house, 1946–1949. In 1947 Suriñach moved to Paris, and in 1951 to New York City, becoming a U.S. citizen in 1959. During 1966–67, he was visiting professor of composition at the Carnegie-Mellon Institute.

Suriñach's contributions to Spanish piano music are few but noteworthy. They include Sonatina, *Flamenquería* (for two pianos), *Trois Chansons et Danses Espagnoles,* and a set of children's pieces entitled *Cuadros flamencos.* The *Three Spanish Songs and Dances* remind one of the successful series by the same title by Mompou. The combining of song and dance, supposedly an old Moorish form, has certainly proved rewarding for both composers.

The first piece of Suriñach's set opens with a striking Andalusian melody in 3/8, accompanied by chords in 3/4. The ensuing dance employs guitar effects with quartal writing and violent chords, typical of the flamenco style. Contrary and parallel figures provide a stirring climax to the dance. The second piece begins with a beautiful cantabile melody that alternates between 3/8 and 4/8. The dance section, very reminiscent of Mompou's Danza No. 5 (also in the key of E major), states a simple, but rhythmically satisfying, tune for a most effective movement. The third work of the series, possibly the most demanding, presents a very atmospheric slow section, bordering on the Impressionistic, followed by a dance that reverts eventually to 3/4 against 3/8. This section is capped off with an *agitato* coda that features swirling patterns of parallel motion in thirds, fourths, tritones, and finally unisons spaced two octaves apart for the stunning conclusion.

The Neoclassic Sonatina proves more difficult, in general, but

not always as idiomatic as the *Songs and Dances*. The first movement is cast in the Scarlattian binary form without repeats, showing
that the eighteenth-century composer still has an impact on Spanish
composers. The second movement is an expressive study in no-
tated trills (five-note groups) for both hands. The finale, marked
presto, has the design of a sonata–rondo, with a main theme of the
perpetual-motion variety.

Gilbert Chase probably best summarizes Suriñach's style when
he states that his music

> achieves an effect of novelty by exploiting all the familiar clichés
> of the "Spanish idiom" with new technical resources and with a
> completely non-Impressionistic sensibility. Sharply etched lines,
> dissonant clashes, emphasis on sheer primitive power of rhythm,
> and strong reliance on percussion give to his music a mid-
> twentieth-century accent that contrasts with the post-
> Impressionistic language prevalent in most contemporary
> Spanish composition. . . . Suriñach brought his disciplined
> technique to bear mainly on the Andalusian idiom, which he
> galvanized into new life by treating it not as romantic atmos-
> phere but as raw material for firmly structured and tautly tex-
> tured scores, in which individual instrumental lines are thrust
> into sharp relief against a strongly percussive rhythmic base.[21]

Summary

The Spanish Civil War and World War II brought a halt to much
of the musical activity in Spain from 1936 to 1945. Since World War
II, Barcelona and Madrid have been the centers of new music for
Spain. In Barcelona (1949), the Manuel de Falla circle promoted
new music, and in Madrid (1958) the Grupo Nueva Música helped
acquaint Spain with some of the newer techniques in composition.
By the 1960s both cities could boast of electronic studios for
musical composition.

Spain was late in being introduced to serial techniques. Rodolfo
Halffter began composing twelve-tone works in the early 1950s but
was living in Mexico after the Civil War. Consequently he did not

have an impact on younger Spanish composers at that time. Later in the 1950s came serial works for keyboard by Luis de Pablo and Cristóbal Halffter. Since that time, numerous Spanish composers have written serial compositions.

After World War II, many Spanish composers began going to Italy and Germany, instead of Paris, to learn new techniques. They sought study and advice from such notables as Luigi Nono, Bruno Maderna, and Karlheinz Stockhausen. Post-serial works for piano have been written by Ramón Barce, Cristóbal Halffter, Luis de Pablo, Carlos Cruz de Castro, Tomás Marco, and Juan Hidalgo, to name only a few.

No less important in this picture of new piano music in Spain is the performer. Pedro Espinosa (b. 1934), originally of Las Palmas, Canary Islands, has become known as one of the most important interpreters of avant-garde piano music, Spanish and otherwise. He has won numerous awards, had many new piano works written especially for him, and has given the first performances of several avant-garde works.

Many of Spain's composers since World War II have purposefully rejected folkloric elements in their music in an attempt to avoid any association with nationalism. They strive or have endeavored to create a more universal musical language with the adoption of serial and post-serial techniques.

Appendix I

Anthologies and Modern Editions of Early Spanish Piano Music

Baciero, Antonio, ed. *Cuadernos para el piano*. Vol. I, *Sonata por la Princesa de Asturias de Antonio Soler (1729–1783)*. Madrid: Real Musical, 1979.

————. *Nueva biblioteca española de música de teclado*. 6 vols., in progress. Madrid: Union Musical Española, 1977–. (Works by Albero and Prieto in Vol. 1; Albero in Vols. 2 and 4; Albero and Prieto in Vol. 5; Albero, Viola?, López, and Anglés in Vol. 6.)

————. *Sebastián de Albero: Sonatas*. 2 vols., in progress. Madrid: Real Musical, 1978–.

Balla, György, ed. *Spanish Piano Music for the Young Musician*. Budapest: Editio Musica, 1974. (Works by M. Albéniz, Cantallos, Casanovas, M. Ferrer, Freixanet, F. Rodríguez, V. Rodríguez, Climent, José, ed. B. Serrano, and Soler.)

Climent, José, ed. *Rafael Anglés: Dos Sonatas*. Madrid: Union Musical Española,. 1970.

Davison, Archibald Thompson, and Apel, Willi, *Historical Anthology of Music*, Vol. 2. Cambridge: Harvard University Press, 1950. (Movement by Blasco de Nebra.)

Doderer, Gerhard, ed. *Spanische und portugiesische Sonaten des 18. Jahrhunderts* (Vol. 6 of *Organa Hispanica*). Heidelberg:

Willy Müller, 1975. (Works by V. Rodríguez, Viola, López, and Soler.)

Donostía, José Antonio, ed. *Música de tecla en el país vasco, siglo XVIII.* San Sebastián, 1953. (Works by Larrañaga, Gamarra, Oxinaga, Echeverria, Sostoa, Biadurre, and Lonbide.)

Kastner, Santiago, ed. *Silva ibérica de música para tecla de los siglos XVI, XVII y XVIII,* Vol. 1. Mainz: Schott, 1954. (Works by Freixanet and Lidón.)

Marchi, Giuliana, ed. *Le più belle pagine dei clavicembalisti spagnoli.* Milan: G. Ricordi, 1955. (Works by V. Rodríguez, Soler, F. Rodríguez, M. Albéniz, Cantallos, and Gallés.)

Newman, William S., ed. *Thirteen Keyboard Sonatas of the 18th and 19th Centuries.* Chapel Hill: The University of North Carolina Press, 1947. (Work by Blasco de Nebra.)

Nin, Joaquín, ed., *Classiques espagnols du piano. Seize sonates . . .* and *Dix-sept sonates et pièces ancienne d'auteurs espagnols.* 2 vols. Paris: Max Eschig, 1925 and 1929. (Works by Soler, M. Albéniz, Cantallos, B. Serrano, and M. Ferrer in Vol. 1; V. Rodríguez, Soler, Freixanet, Casanovas, Anglés, F. Rodríguez, and Gallés in Vol. 2.)

Parris, Robert, ed. *Manuel Blasco de Nebra: Seis sonatas para clave, y fuerte piano, Op. 1.* Madrid: Union Musical Española, 1964.

Pedrell, Felipe, ed. *Antologia de Organistas Clasicos Españoles (siglos XVI, XVII y XVIII).* 2 vols. Madrid: I. Alier, 1908. (Work by Juan Moreno y Polo in Vol. 2.)

———. *Salterio Sacro-Hispano.* Barcelona: Manuel Salvat. A series of vocal and keyboard music. (A work by J. Moreno y Polo, No. 119 of the series; a work by Anselmo Viola, No. 124 of the series.)

Powell, Linton, ed. *Joaquin Montero: Seis sonatas para clave y fuerte piano, Op. 1.* Madrid: Union Musical Española, 1977.

Pujol, David, ed. *Mestres de l'escolania de Montserrat, Música instrumental.* 2 vols. Monestir de Montserrat, 1934. (Works by Casanovas in Vol. 1; F. Rodríguez and Vinyals in Vol. 2.)

Rubio, Samuel, ed. *Antonio Soler: Sonatas para instrumentos de tecla.* 7 vols. Madrid: Union Musical Española, 1957–1972.

Ruiz-Pipó, Antonio, ed. *Joaquin Montero: Diez minuetes para clave y fuerte piano.* Madrid: Union Musical Española, 1973.

————. *Música vasca del siglo XVIII para tecla.* Madrid: Union Musical Española, 1972. (Works by Oxinaga, Larrañaga, Gamarra, Echeverria, Lonbide, Sostoa, and Eguiguren.)

Appendix II

Spanish Piano Music since World War II: A Selective List with Publishers

Alfonso, Javier. *Suite (Homenaje a Isaac Albéniz)*. Madrid: Union Musical Española, © 1966.

Barce, Ramón. *Estudio de Densidades*. Madrid: Editorial de Música Española Contemporánea, © 1974.

Benguerel, Xavier. *Suite*. Barcelona: Editorial Boileau, © 1959.

Blancafort, Alberto. *Sonata*. Madrid: Union Musical Española, © 1960.

Cano, Francisco. *Continuo*. Madrid: Editorial de Música Española Contemporánea, © 1974.

Carra, Manuel. *Cuatro piezas breves*. Madrid: Union Musical Española, © 1960.

Castillo, Manuel. *Preludio, Diferencias y Toccata (sobre un tema de Isaac Albéniz)*. Madrid: Union Musical Española, © 1962.

Cercós, Josep. *Sonata*. Barcelona: Ediciones Armonico, © 1954.

Coria, Miguel Ángel. *Dos piezas para piano*. Madrid: Editorial de Música Española Contemporánea, © 1974.

Cruz de Castro, Carlos. *Domino-Klavier*. Madrid: Editorial Alpuerto, © 1970.

———. *Llámalo como quieras*. Madrid: Editorial de Música Española Contemporánea, © 1974.

García Abril, Anton. *Sonatina*. Madrid: Union Musical Española, © 1957.

González Acilu, Agustin. *Presencias*. Madrid: Editorial de Música Española Contemporánea, © 1967.

Guinjoan, Joan. *Celulas No. 1*. Madrid: Editorial de Música Española Contemporánea, © 1975.

Halffter, Cristóbal. *Sonata*. Madrid: Union Musical Española, © 1953.

———. *Introduccion, Fuga y Final*. Madrid: Union Musical Española, © 1959.

Halffter, Ernesto. *Preludio y Danza*. Madrid: Union Musical Española, © 1974.

Halffter, Rodolfo. *Tercera Sonata*. © 1968 by the composer. Available through Ediciones Mexicanas de Música, Mexico, D.F.

———. *Laberinto*. © 1972 by the composer. Available through Ediciones Mexicanas de Música, Mexico, D.F.

Hidalgo, Juan. *Milan Piano*. Madrid: Editorial de Música Española Contemporánea, © 1974.

Marco, Tomás. *Temporalia*. Celle: Moeck, © 1974.

———. *Fetiches*. Madrid: Editorial de Música Española Contemporánea, © 1977.

Mompou, Federico. *Música callada*. Paris: Editions Salabert, © 1959.

———. *Variations sur un thème de Chopin*. Paris: Editions Salabert, © 1961.

Montsalvatge, Xavier. *Tres Divertimentos*. New York: Southern Music Publishing Co., © 1955.

———. *Sonatine Pour Yvette*. Paris: Editions Salabert, © 1962.

Moreno Gans, José. *Homenaje a Albéniz*. Madrid: Union Musical Española, © 1962.

Nin-Culmell, Joaquín. *Tonadas*. New York: Rongwen Music, Inc., © 1957.

Oliver, Ángel. *Psicograma No. 1*. Madrid: Editorial Alpuerto, © 1971.

Pablo, Luis de. *Sonata, Op. 3*. Madrid: Union Musical Española, © 1960.

Prieto, Claudio. *Juguetes para pianistas*. Madrid: Editorial Alpuerto, © 1974.

Soler, Josep. *Tres peçes per a piano*. New York: Southern Music Publishing Co., Inc. © 1970.

Suriñach, Carlos. *Trois Chansons et Danses Espagnoles*. New York: Peer-International Corporation, © 1953.
————. *Sonatina*. New York: Peer-International Corporation, © 1959.
Villa Rojo, Jesús. *Nueve piezas breves*. Madrid: Editorial Alpuerto, © 1968–1969.

Glossary

Rhythmic patterns given for the dances serve only as examples; there are many variants.

acciaccatura. Literally a "crushing" tone. A keyboard ornament that requires the playing, together with the normal note, of its neighboring tone, which is to be released immediately.

Alberti bass. Named for Domenico Alberti (1710–1740?). A keyboard accompaniment for the left hand consisting of a broken-chord pattern of four notes.

appoggiatura. Literally a "leaning" tone. A rhythmically strong dissonant note occurring in place of a harmonic note.

bolero. Dance in triple time, characterized by a triplet on the first weak beat of the measure; more deliberate in tempo than the *seguidilla*.

bulerías. A lively *flamenco* song and dance in 3/8.

cante. Song or singing, usually referring to an Andalusian gipsy song.

cante jondo. Literally "deep song." A highly emotional and tragic song of Andalusia.

copla. Couplet, stanza, or popular song. In reference to Spanish piano music, usually the lyrical melody that contrasts with the more rhythmic parts of the piece.

fandango. Old Spanish dance with strongly marked triple time. Other varieties include the *malagueña, granadina, murciana,* and *rondeña.*

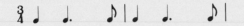

fandanguillo. A little *fandango.*

flamenco. An Andalusian type of song and dance performed by trained singers and dancers to the accompaniment of a guitar. Some of the varieties include *malagueñas, peteneras,* and *bulerías.*

galant style. See *style galant.*

guajira. Spanish Cuban dance with a characteristic shift from 6/8 to 3/4.

habanera. Dance of Havana, in slow to moderate duple meter. Probably Hispanic in origin and reimported to Spain with an exotic tinge. Similar to the *tango.*

hemiola. Time values in the relationship 3:2, e.g.,

jota. Dance form that appears in many variants throughout Spain. The *jota aragonesa* is in fast triple time and characterized by triplets.

malagueña. Song and dance from Málaga. Derived from the *fandango* and in 3/4 time.

paso doble.   A kind of one-step (though the name means "double step") in 6/8 that became popular about 1926.

petenera.   Andalusian dance characterized by the alternation of 3/4 and 3/8.

polo.   Andalusian dance in triple meter, with frequent syncopations of the hemiola type.

punteado.   In guitar music, notes played in succession, as opposed to *rasgueado.*

rasgueado.   In guitar playing, strumming the strings with a finger to produce arpeggios and chordal effects.

ricercar.   Generally associated with instrumental music of the sixteenth and seventeenth centuries. The commonest type of *ricercar* employed imitative treatment of one or more themes.

rondeña.   A variety of the *fandango* from the region around Ronda.

saeta.   Andalusian folksong sung during Lent or the Feast of the Nativity to accompany street processions and other outdoor devotional activities.

sardana.   National dance of Cataluña, usually in quick 6/8 time.

schottische.   Mid-nineteenth-century round dance similar to a slow polka.

seguidilla.   Highly popular dance and song in a quick triple meter. Several types are to be found, e.g., *seguidillas sevillanas,* of Seville.

siguiriya gitana. Andalusian gipsy dance, possibly from "seguidilla," marked by the alternation of 3/8 and 3/4.

soleares (soleá). From *soledad* ("solitude"). Gipsy–Andalusian plaintive song of sorrow and loneliness.

style galant. In the eighteenth century, the light, elegant style of the rococo in contrast to the more serious, elaborate style of the Baroque.

tarantas. Folk song/dance related to the *malagueña*, but from the region of Almería and Murcia.

tiento. The Iberian counterpart of the Italian *ricercar*. The *tiento* originated with *vihuela* music and was later used for organ music characterized by imitative counterpoint.

tirana. Andalusian dance/song in moderate triple meter.

tonadilla. From the middle of the eighteenth century to the early nineteenth century, a short, popular, comic opera, with one to four characters, consisting of solo song and occasional choruses.

vihuela. A Spanish-type lute of the sixteenth century. Its tuning was similar to that of the lute but it had a guitar-like body.

zambra. The same as the Arab word *sâmira*, which was used by the Moors in Spain to mean "revelry by night."

zapateado. Dance in quick time with marked heel stampings.

zarzuela. Spanish-style opera, distinguished from regular opera in that the music is intermingled with spoken dialogue, as in comic opera. Its name comes from the palace outside Madrid named La Zarzuela.

zortziko. Basque folk dance in dotted rhythm in a quick 5/8.

Notes

1. Early Spanish Piano Music, 1740–1840

1. According to Ferguson/*Keyboard*, p.5, the clavichord remained in use in Spain until the early nineteenth century, largely as a practice instrument for organists, and sometimes with a separate pedalboard attached. The term *clavicordio* indicated harpsichord. Clavichord was designated in Spain by the term *monacordio*.

2. Chase/*Spain*, pp.127–128.

3. Anglès/*Catálogo* I:330–333.

4. The major editions of Scarlatti's sonatas include *Opere complete per clavicembalo*, ed. Alessandro Longo (Milan: Ricordi, 1907–1937); *Sixty Sonatas Edited in Chronological Order*, ed. Ralph Kirkpatrick (New York: G. Schirmer, 1953); *Sonatas*, ed. Kenneth Gilbert (Paris: Heugel, 1971–); *Complete Keyboard Works in Facsimile* (from the Manuscript and Printed Sources), ed. Ralph Kirkpatrick (New York: Johnson, 1972). "K" and "L" numbers refer to Kirkpatrick and Longo numbers, respectively.

5. For more recent research on Scarlatti, see Sheveloff/"Scarlatti."

6. Thomas Roseingrave (1690–1766), English printer and composer, was a friend of Scarlatti's from their days in Rome.

7. Kirkpatrick/*Scarlatti*, pp.252–253.

8. Ibid., p.256.

9. For a discussion of the use of the crux in some twentieth-century Spanish sonatas, see Powell/"Halffter."

10. Recall that the pianoforte was invented in 1709 by the Italian Bartolomeo Cristofori.

11. Kirkpatrick/*Scarlatti*, pp.178–184.

12. Apparently some of Scarlatti's later sonatas do not feature difficult hand-crossings because he became too fat to cross his hands at the harpsichord. See Scholes/*Burney*, pp.86–87.

13. For futher discussion of guitar effects in Scarlatti's sonatas, see chapter 4.

14. Scholes/*Burney*, p.87.

15. I am indebted to Jane Clark for providing me with much information regarding the influence of Spanish folk music on Scarlatti's sonatas. See Clark/"Scarlatti," pp.19–21.

16. Newman/*SCE*, p.279.

17. Nin tells us in his preface to Vol. II that this sonata comes from a manuscript notebook belonging to the Spanish composer Eduardo López Chavarri (1871–1970). This sonata is also published in Marchi/ *Clavicembalisti*.

18. Almonte Howell, "The Sonatas of Vincente Rodríguez, A Preliminary Report," paper presented at the meeting of the South Central Chapter of the American Musicological Society, Danville, Kentucky, April 1, 1977.

19. "Book of Toccatas for the Harpsichord distributed over all the keynotes of the octave, with the proviso that those based on white keys occur with both major and minor thirds, while those on black keys are excepted, and because of the out-of-tuneness of various of the scale degrees, occur only in the least ill-sounding form" (translation by Almonte Howell). We can note from the title that this collection represents a partial "Well-Tempered Clavier," similar to J.K.F. Fischer's *Ariadne musica*.

20. This sonata has been published in Doderer/*Spanische*.

21. From the preface to Climent/*Anglés*.

22. According to *Diccionario Labor* I:79, Anglés was organist of the Valencia Cathedral only from 1762 to 1772.

23. These works are extracts from a manuscript belonging to the noted Spanish pianist José Iturbi. See Nin/*Classiques* II:ii.

24. According to Climent, the markings in the first seven measures are from the manuscript.

25. Baciero/*Nueva Biblioteca* I:vii states that Albero was appointed first organist of the Royal Chapel in 1748, but Baciero/*Albero* I:vii gives the date as 1746.

26. Parrish/"Piano," p.255.

27. Thus far only two works by this title, out of a projected six, have been made available in Baciero/*Nueva Biblioteca* I and II.

28. The Albero sonatas are located in the Biblioteca Nazionale Marciana, Venice. Baciero/*Albero* I:ix gives possible dates of the works as 1755–1756.

29. Fourteen of these sonatas are now available in modern edition. See Baciero/*Albero*.

30. Sheveloff/"Scarlatti," p.450.

31. Baciero promises more information on Albero in Baciero/*Albero* II.

32. See Nin/*Classiques* I:iv.

33. Thanks to the efforts of Samuel Rubio, seven volumes (120 sonatas) of Soler are available, published by Union Musical Española, Madrid, 1957–1972; these volumes give the sources of the surviving manuscripts. "R" numbers refer to the Rubio edition. Frederick Marvin has also edited several volumes of Soler sonatas, which are published by Mills Music, Inc. In addition, fourteen sonatas can be found in Nin/*Classiques*—twelve in Vol. I, and two in Vol. II—but all with editorial emendations. A newly discovered sonata by Soler, *Sonata por la Princesa de Asturias,* has been published by Antonio Baciero. See Baciero/*Cuadernos* I.

34. For a more detailed discussion of the Soler sonatas, see Newman/ *SCE,* pp.279–285.

35. For example, see volumes IV and VI of the Rubio edition.

36. For more information on this treatise and Soler's application of his modulatory techniques in his sonatas and other works, see Carroll/ "Soler."

37. Newman/*SCE,* p.283.

38. See *Enciclopedia universal* 44:449. I am grateful to Jean R. Longland of the Hispanic Society of America for calling this information to my attention.

39. These few works by Oxinaga, who was possibly of Basque origin, are published in Ruiz-Pipó/*Música vasca.*

40. Preface to Howell/*Sessé.*

41. Saldoni/*Diccionario* II:117–118. Another collection, *Quaderno primero de una coleccion de piezas de música para clavicordio, forte-piano, y órgano,* is mentioned in Espinosa/"López," p.382.

42. The sole surviving copy of the eighteenth-century edition is now at the Brussels Royal Library. A modern edition, edited by Almonte Howell, is published by Union Musical Española.

43. Preface to Howell/*Sessé.*

44. A striking portrait of Félix Máximo López, done by the court painter Vicente López (1772–1850), now hangs at the Casón del Buen Retiro, an annex of the Prado Museum in Madrid.

45. Espinosa/"López," pp.127–132.

46. Ibid., abstract.

47. Gillespie/"López," p.247.

48. Kastner/*Silva ibérica* I gives Lidón's birth date as 1752, but *Diccionario Labor* II:1409 cites 1746 with documentation.

49. Listed in *Diccionario Labor* II:1409.

50. Nin/*Classiques* I:i.

51. Published in Kastner/*Silva ibériea* I. Kastner informs us that this work comes from a collection of manuscripts of the eighteenth and early nineteenth centuries owned by the Reverend Cándido Ledesma Santos, organist of Ciudad Rodrigo Cathedral. The collection was later donated to the archive of that church.

52. Preface to Kastner/*Silva ibérica* I.
53. Newman/*SCE*, p.311.
54. A musical example from these four-hand sonatas can be found in Mitjana/"Espagne," pp.2286–2287.
55. Both sets of sonatas are available in modern edition, published by Union Musical Española of Madrid. See Powell/*Montero;* and Parris/ *Blasco de Nebra.*
56. *Librarian's Report of the Library of Congress*, 1940; and *Diccionario Labor* I:303.
57. See also Saldoni/*Diccionario* III:191–193.
58. Ibid., IV:215–216.
59. These minuets are published by Union Musical Española. See Ruiz-Pipó/*Montero.*
60. Recall the earlier Albero *Obras para clavicordio o piano forte,* written between 1746 and 1756.
61. Newman/*SCE*, pp.306–307.
62. Kirkpatrick/*Scarlatti,* p.205.
63. Newman/*SCE*, pp.309–310.
64. Unfortunately, I have been unable to locate Donostía/*Música de tecla,* but according to Espinosa/"López," pp.382–383, sonatas by the following eighteenth-century Basque composers can be found in the anthology: José Larrañaga, Manuel Gamarra, Joaquin de Oxinaga, Joaquin Echeverria, Manuel de Sostoa, José Biadurre, and Juan Lonbide. Donostía/*Música y Musicos*, pp.76–78 also lists Basque composers of the eighteenth century and some of their works.
65. Ruiz-Pipó/*Música vasca,* pp.vi-vii.
66. Ibid., p.vii.
67. Pedrell/*Diccionario,* p.675; and *Diccionario Labor* I:899.
68. Pedrell/*Catàlech* II:311. Baciero/*Cuadernos* I:12 lists four sonatas by Ferrer. These works are among several by various composers from a MS dated 1776.
69. Nin/*Classiques* I:v; and Saldoni/*Diccionario* II:574.
70. Published in Nin/*Classiques* I and Marchi/*Clavicembalisti.* Nin tells us that it is part of a manuscript that includes sonatas by Soler, Haydn, Edelmann, and an unidentified son of J.S. Bach.
71. Fétis/*Biographie universelle,* p.120. See also Saldoni/*Diccionario* I:297 and IV:263.
72. A Sonata in F and a Sonata in G major are projected for Vol. III and Vol. V of the Baciero series, respectively.
73. Pedrell/*Salterio* (No. 124 of the series) contains a Sonatina by Anselmo Viola that is the same as the first movement of F. Rodríguez's Sonata in F minor, No. 6 in Pujol/*Mestres* II.
74. Fétis/*Biographie universelle,* Suppl. II:631.
75. Saldoni/*Diccionario* II:206–207.
76. Newman/*SCE*, p.286, refers to them as clarinet sonatas, but they are

sonatas for the trumpets of the Spanish organ, as in Soler's *Sonata de clarines*.

77. Published in Pujol/*Mestres* I. Sonata No. 4 of this collection is also published in Nin/*Classiques* II.

78. Published in Pujol/*Mestres* II. The Rondo in B-flat major is also published in Nin/*Classiques* II and Marchi/*Clavicembalisti*. Nin mentions that he had two manuscript versions of the Rondo, one from Madrid and one from Barcelona. He printed the Madrid version, stating that "the Barcelona version includes between measures 94 and 95 a short digression of nine measures which spoils the unity of this exquisite piece." The other version can be seen in Pujol/*Mestres* II.

79. Published in Pujol/*Mestres* II.

80. Newman/*SCE*, p.313.

81. Nin/*Classiques* II, original manuscripts in the Biblioteca de Catalunya.

82. Kastner/*Silva ibérica* I, original manuscript in the library of the Orfeó Català.

83. For a detailed discussion of the *style galant*, see Newman/*SCE*, pp. 120–122.

84. Frederick Marvin also has published this work but contends that it is by Soler (*Sonatas for Piano*, Vol. III [London: Mills Music Ltd., 1959]). Marvin states that the manuscript in the Biblioteca de Catalunya in Barcelona is earlier than 1795 (date given by Nin) and is clearly by Soler. Baciero/*Cuadernos* I:12: also lists a sonata by Cantallos from a manuscript dated 1776 that contains works by various composers.

85. Newman/*SCE*, p.311.

86. Published in Nin/*Classiques* I.

87. Ibid., I:vi.

88. Newman/*SCE*, p.311.

89. Mitjana/"Espagne," p.2185. Pedrell/*Salterio* (No. 119 of the series) lists a Sonatina (1755) by J. Moreno y Polo, and Pedrell/*Antologia* II contains a Sonatina (1776) by Juan Moreno. *Libro músico de canto de órgano compuesto por diferentes autores*, 1776, lists a Sonata by Moreno (see Baciero/*Cuadernos* I:12).

90. According to *Enciclopedia universal* 36:1023. See also Gómez/*Latassa* II:366.

91. Sonatas Nos. 2, 3, 6, 7, 10, and 16 (as numbered in the MS) were published in Nin/*Classiques* II. Sonatas Nos. 3 and 16 were also published in Marchi/*Clavicembalisti* without, of course, Nin's editorial emendations.

92. Newman/*SCE*, p.313.

93. Saldoni/*Diccionario* I:89–106.

94. Nin/*Classiques* I:vi.

2. **The Piano Music of Isaac Albéniz, Enrique Granados,
Their Immediate Predecessors, and Their Contemporaries**

1. Nin/*Classiques* I:vi.
2. The *Estudios* are published by Union Musical Española.
3. Mitjana/"Espagne," p.2325; and Salazar/*El Siglo*, p.101.
4. Mitjana/"Espagne," p.2325; Salazar/*El Siglo*, p.101; *Diccionario Labor* I:26.
5. Henri Herz (1803–1888) and Friedrich Kalkbrenner (1785–1849) were two of the fashionable salon pianists in Paris during the early nineteenth century.
6. An autographed copy is available at the Biblioteca Musical of Madrid, as cited in *CBM*.
7. Sigismond Thalberg (1812–1871), sometimes called "old arpeggio," was the greatest rival of Liszt. Thalberg delighted in astounding audiences with his new trick of bringing out a melody with both thumbs in the middle register of the piano and enveloping that melody with arpeggios so that it sounded as if more than one person were playing.
8. Eslava/"Albéniz" gives a complete list of P. Albéniz's works.
9. The fantasias on themes from *I Puritani* and *Lucia di Lammermoor* can be found in the Biblioteca Nacional in Madrid.
10. See Friedheim/"Liszt."
11. Mitjana/"Espagne," p.2287.
12. Salazar/*El Siglo*, pp.99–100.
13. According to Subirá/*Historia*, pp.640–641, there is a *Biografía de don Santiago de Masarnáu* by José María Quadrado; some of Masarnáu's works can be found in the library of the Madrid Conservatory, and his *Tesoro del pianista* is in the Biblioteca Nacional.
14. *Enciclopedia universal* 24:321.
15. Miró's date of birth is given as 1810 in Espin/"Miró," p.83. Saldoni/*Diccionario* III:80 and Parada y Barreto/*Diccionario* p.273, give it as 1815.
16. Espin/"Miró," p.83.
17. Ibid.
18. Saldoni/*Diccionario* III:82.
19. As cited in the *Gaceta Musical de Madrid*, December 28, 1865, pp. 53–54; Fétis/*Biographie universelle* V:248; Parada y Barreto/*Diccionario*, p.249; and Saldoni/*Diccionario* III:20–21.
20. A copy of the *Repertorio orgánico* is in the Biblioteca Nacional in Madrid.
21. For more information on this term associated with musical Romanticism, see Longyear/*Romanticism*, p.274.
22. Gillespie/*Keyboard Music*, p.316.
23. Pierre Zimmerman was head of the piano department at the Paris Conservatory 1820–1848.

24. Saldoni/*Diccionario* I:251–252.
25. These works can be found in the Biblioteca Nacional in Madrid.
26. These works are also located at the Biblioteca Nacional.
27. Parada y Barreto/*Diccionario*, pp.259–260.
28. *Diccionario Labor* I:1167.
29. Aranguren's piano method is advertised several times in the 1864 edition of *El Orfeon Español*, which states that it was adopted by the Real Conservatorio of Madrid as well as the Escolania of Montserrat. Copies of the method book can be found in the Biblioteca Musical in Madrid.
30. *Diccionario Labor* I:94.
31. Ibid., I:13.
32. According to Subirá/*Historia*, p.642, Adalid wrote waltzes, ballades, elegies, fantasies, nocturnes, romances without words, and mazurkas.
33. Ibid., p.643.
34. *Enciclopedia universal* 48:999–1000.
35. Many works by Zabalza are given in *CBM*, and a copy of the Sonatinas is in the Biblioteca Nacional.
36. Subirá/*Historia*, p.644.
37. Pedrell/*Diccionario*, p.397. The piano method is cited in *CBM*.
38. *Diccionario Labor* II:1811.
39. The Biblioteca Nacional in Madrid preserves many works for piano by Pujol.
40. Reprinted in *Gaceta Musical de Madrid,* November 30, and December 7, 1865.
41. Mayer-Serra/"Nationalism," pp.1–2.
42. See also Collet/*L'Essor*, pp.36–41.
43. The last three works are in the Biblioteca Nacional in Madrid. *Cantos canarios* is published by Union Musical Española.
44. Subirá/*Historia*, p.665, notes that Montalbán was considered by some in Spain as the best author of didactic works for the piano.
45. The folk song "El Vito" was also used by Joaquin Turina in his *Sonata romántica*, Op. 3, and by Manuel Infante for a set of variations for piano.
46. Subirá/*Historia*, p.697.
47. Hamilton/"Serrano," p.718.
48. *CBM* cites *Figuras abreviadas de adorno, Escuela de piano*, and *Mazurka melódica. Diccionario Labor* II:2137 mentions a *zortzico*.
49. This work is in the Biblioteca Nacional in Madrid.
50. Other smaller works by Nicolau can be found in the Biblioteca Nacional. *CBM* lists an *Allegretto*.
51. "Danse Triste" from Noguera's set of *Trois danses. . .* can be found in Clough-Leighter/*Album*.
52. According to *Diccionario Labor* II:1639.

53. Trend/"Alió." See also Nadal/"Alió."
54. This Catalan folk song was also used by Federico Mompou in his piano piece *Canción y Danza IV*.
55. Collet/*L'Essor*, p.42; and *Diccionario Labor* II:1664. The Library of Congress possesses a copy of the *Sonate Espagnole*, which is listed as Olmeda's second sonata. I have been unable to locate a first sonata. The preface to the second sonata states that it was written some years earlier, but that it was revised in 1906.
56. The sardanas *La Santa Espina* and *La Nit de L'Amor* are published by Union Musical Española.
57. *Diccionario Labor* II:1380. Numerous works by Larregla can be found in the Biblioteca Nacional and Biblioteca Musical of Madrid.
58. *¡Viva Navarra!* is published by Union Musical Española. The final three measures of unsatisfactory trills (in the Zozaya edition) have been changed to a more suitable close.
59. *Oriental* can be found in Clough-Leighter/*Album*, and the Sonata is listed in *CBM*.
60. According to Mast/"Albéniz." However, Marliave/*Études*, p.121, cites 500; Van Vechten/*Excavations*, pp.241–242, gives 500–600; and Villar/*Músicos* I:75 states 900. These figures more than likely refer to the number of works composed, rather than published. For an extensive list of Albéniz's piano works, see the appendix of Mast/"Albéniz."
61. Mellers/"Mompou," pp.46–47.
62. Newman/*SSB*, p.652.
63. Ibid., p.653.
64. Collet/*L'Essor*, pp.55–56.
65. The *jota* exists in various forms associated with different regions of Spain. Two examples of the non-Hispanic cultivation of the *jota* deserve mention: Liszt's *Rhapsodie Espagnole (Folies d'Espagne et Jota Aragonesa)* is complete with arabesques and pyrotechnics in the typical Lisztian manner; and Gottschalk's *La Jota Aragonesa* is one of serveral works by this nineteenth-century composer to employ Spanish dance rhythms.
66. Istel/"Albéniz," p.142.
67. Ibid.
68. According to Starkie/*Spain* II:122.
69. Chase/*Spain*, p.157.
70. *Cante jondo* (literally "deep song") is a traditional song form of Andalusia.
71. Chase/*Spain*, pp.157–158.
72. Quoted in Gillespie/*Keyboard Music*, p.318.
73. Mast/"Albéniz," p.363.
74. Other examples of this chord can be found in *Málaga* (mm. 11–12) and *Jerez* (mm. 202–203).
75. Quoted in Chase/*Spain*, p.159.

76. Mast/"Albéniz," p.368.
77. One of Granados's most distinguished pupils was Frank Marshall, later to become the director of the Academia Granados. The present director, Alicia de Larrocha, a pupil of Marshall, is one of the most praised interpreters of Granados's works.
78. Chase/*Spain*, p.161.
79. According to Larrocha/"Granados," pp.22–23. Fairly complete lists of Granados's piano works can be found in *Grove* 5, III:756 and in *Revista Musical Catalana* 13 (1916):208–209. The latter also contains a list of memorial concerts given in April and May of 1916, only a matter of weeks after Granados's death.
80. Livermore/"Granados," p.87.
81. Quoted in Gillespie/*Keyboard Music*, p.321; and Larrocha/"Granados," p.23.
82. The *majos* and *majas* were the members of Madrid's lower classes in Goya's time.
83. Blas de Laserna (1751–1816) was an important composer of *tonadillas* in Spain. The *Tirana del Trípili* is given in Mitjana/"Espagne," pp. 2290–2291.
84. Pedro Albéniz also made use of this famous song in two rondos written earlier in the nineteenth century.
85. Chase/*Spain*, p.164.
86. Ibid.
87. See Newman/*SSB* 139.
88. Cited in Gillespie/*Keyboard Music*, p.323.
89. Newman/"Goyescas," p.347.
90. Quoted in Chase/*Spain*, p.165.

3. Falla, Turina, Mompou, and Their Contemporaries

1. Pahissa/*Falla*, p.35.
2. Crowder/"Falla," p.11.
3. Ibid., p.13.
4. According to Wirth/"Falla," p.1751, this work was written in Madrid in 1903. Apparently it is still unpublished.
5. Originally entitled *Pour le tombeau de Paul Dukas*, this work first appeared in the musical supplement of *La Revue Musicale*, May–June 1936, pp.7–9.
6. Chase/"Falla," pp.41–42.
7. Ibid., p.43.
8. Esteban/"Falla," p.19.
9. Chase/"Falla," p.46.
10. Sopeña/*Turina*, pp.22–23.
11. Ibid., pp.35–36.

12. Starkie/*Spain* II:129.

13. Ibid., p.130.

14. For detailed information on Turina's piano music and a complete list of his works for piano, see Powell/"Turina." Though *Fantasía del reloj*, Op. 94, is listed in the appendix of Sopeña/*Turina*, it has never been published.

15. Sopeña/*Turina*, p.88.

16. Lockwood/*Notes*, p.192.

17. Quoted in Sopeña/*Turina*, p.43.

18. Dean/"Turina," p.95.

19. Although the MS of the work has been lost, the various movements are listed in the appendix of Sopeña/*Turina*.

20. For more information on the influence of dance rhythms on Turina's piano music, see Powell/"Rhythms."

21. Falla also paid homage to Arbós with his "Fanfare on the Name E. F. Arbós," from *Homenajes*.

22. For more information on this work, see Powell/"Nationalists."

23. For a pedagogical discussion of the initial movement of *El circo*, see Bryant/"Lesson," pp.21–26.

24. Dean/"Turina," p.96.

25. Starkie/*Spain* II:130.

26. *Musical Times* 72 (1931):515.

27. *Monthly Musical Record* 42 (1932):113.

28. Trend/"Falla," pp.11–12.

29. For more information on Turina's melodic style, see Powell/"Spain."

30. Chase/"Esplá," p.199. The noted English scholar of Spanish music John Trend gives a lengthy discussion on "The Spanish Idiom" in Trend/*Spanish*.

31. Chase/"Esplá," p.200.

32. Bergerac/"Andalusian," pp.162–163.

33. Dean/"Turina," p.96.

34. For a more detailed discussion of this sonata, see Powell/"Cyclical."

35. For more detailed biographical information on Mompou, see Janés/*Mompou*.

36. Huot/"Mompou," p.77.

37. Mellers/"Mompou," p.47.

38. Vuillermoz/*Musiques*, pp.123–125.

39. Mellers/"Mompou," p.47.

40. Huot/"Mompou," p.58.

41. Starkie/*Spain* II:134. For a complete list of works by Mompou, see the appendixes of Iglesias/*Mompou* and Janés/*Mompou*.

42. Quoted in *Grove 5*, V:825.

43. To date there are fourteen works in this series. No. 13, however, is

for guitar, and No. 14 is unpublished. No. 14 was written especially for the concert celebrating the composer's 85th birthday. It was given at Alice Tully Hall, Lincoln Center for the Performing Arts, New York, March 26, 1978.

44. Reference to each folk song used, with complete text in Catalan and Castilian, is given in Iglesias/*Mompou*, pp.225–280. See also Méeus/"Mompou."

45. Iglesias/*Mompou*, p.303.

46. From San Juan de la Cruz, *Cántico espiritual*. See Janés/*Mompou*, p.248.

47. Janés/*Mompou*, p.255.

48. Huot/"Mompou," p.58.

49. Starkie/"Mompou," p.826.

50. Another work, *Para la tumba de Lenin* (1937), has remained in MS.

51. See Kirkpatrick/*Scarlatti*, p.90.

52. Powell/"Halffter," p.4.

53. Ibid., p.5.

54. Field/"Halffter," p.7.

55. *Music Review* 10 (1949):127.

56. For more information on the bagatelles, see Field/"Bagatelas."

57. For more detailed information on the second sonata, see Field/"Segunda Sonata."

58. Field/"Halffter," p.7.

59. Chase/*Spain*, p.202.

60. Ibid., p.317.

61. Ibid., p.205.

62. Salazar/*Música*, p.249.

63. Ibid., p.262.

64. Pittaluga was on the staff of the Spanish Embassy in Washington, 1937–1939, after which he went to France.

65. Reprinted in *Musicalia* (Havana), Nos. 15–16, January–April 1931.

66. Chase/*Spain*, p.203.

67. For more biographical information, see Borrás/*Conrado del Campo*.

68. Salazar/*Música*, p.223.

69. Ibid., pp.223–224.

70. Collet/*L'Essor*, p.146.

71. *Diccionario Labor* I:1026.

72. Ibid.

73. Chase/*Spain*, p.169.

74. *Diccionario Labor* II:1466.

75. See Collet/*L'Essor*, p.149; and Valls/*Música*, pp.133–137.

76. *Diccionario Labor* I:98.

77. Valls/*Música*, p.150.

78. Collet/*L'Essor*, p.129.

79. For more information on Palau, see Fernández-Cid/*Música*, pp. 83–88; and Mingote/*Palau*.

80. For a more detailed discussion of these works, except for *Homenaje a Debussy*, see Leon Tello/*Palau*.

81. Ibid., p.45.

82. Sopeña/*Rodrigo*, pp.133–134, gives a complete list of works through 1946. Sopeña/*Historia*, pp.376–377, and *Diccionario Labor* II:1898 list piano works through 1952.

83. Diego/*Música*, p.183.

84. Collet/*L'Essor*, p.97. Chase/*Spain*, pp.173–174, gives the scale incorrectly as C–D-flat–E-flat–E-natural–F–G-flat–A-flat–B-flat.

85. Fernández-Cid/*Música*, p.80; and Collet/*L'Essor*, p.97.

86. Collet/*L'Essor*, p.97.

87. For a list of Esplá's piano works, see Sopeña/*Historia*, p.354.

88. Salazar/*Música*, p.236.

89. Chase/"Esplá," pp.199–203.

90. *Obras musicales del Padre Donostia* (Lecaroz, Navarra: Archivo Padre Donostia, 1960–).

91. For a complete list of Guridi's works, see the appendix of Arozamena/*Guridi*.

92. Fernández-Cid/*Música*, p.145.

93. Chase/*Spain*, p.179.

94. For a complete list, see Arozamena/*Usandizaga*, pp.366–367. Brief comments on some of the piano works can be found in Arozamena/*Usandizaga*, pp.159–161.

95. Fernández-Cid/*Música*, pp.158–162. For more information on García Leoz, see Fernández-Cid/*Música*, pp.187–203.

96. Chase/*Spain*, p.178.

97. Collet/*L'Essor*, p.103.

98. The song "El Vito" can be found in Vol. 2 of *Vingt chants populaires*, edited by Joaquin Nin.

99. Sonata (1934) was originally published by Oxford University Press. The title was changed to *Sonata breve* when it was reissued by Broude Brothers in 1955.

100. Lourié/"Musings," p.241.

101. Ellis/"Character Piece," p.682–683.

4. The Influence of the Guitar on Spanish Keyboard Music

1. Chase/"Falla," p.43.

2. Kirkpatrick/*Scarlatti*, p.205.

3. Chase/*Spain*, p.114.

4. Kirkpatrick/*Scarlatti*, p.205.

5. Chase/*Spain*, p.114.

6. Chase/"Falla," p.43.

7. A complete list of Turina's piano works that employ guitar effects can be found in Powell/"Guitar Effects," p.42; and Powell/"Turina," p.166.

8. Trend/*Spanish*, p.97.
9. Quoted in *Grove 5*, VII:198.

5. **Spanish Piano Music since World War II**

1. Marco/"Traditionalism," p.41.
2. Vinton/*Dictionary*, p.791.
3. Valls/*Música*, p.202.
4. Ibid., p.201.
5. Vinton/*Dictionary*, pp.478–479. For more information on Mestres Quadreny, see Wolf-Eberhard von Lewinski, "Vier katalanische Komponisten in Barcelona," *Melos* 38 (1971):92–103.
6. Marco/*Música*, pp.48–49.
7. For more biographical information see Franco/*Montsalvatge*.
8. Vinton/*Dictionary*, p.495.
9. Valls/*Música*, p.160.
10. Franco/*Montsalvatge*, p.61.
11. See also René Leibowitz, "La música de Xavier Benguerel," *Serra d'or* 101(1968):68–70; and Wolf-Eberhard von Lewinski, "Vier katalanische Komponisten in Barcelona," *Melos* 38 (1971):92–103.
12. Custer/"Contemporary," p.53.
13. Fernández-Cid/*Música*, p.198.
14. Custer/"Contemporary," p.53.
15. From an interview with Otto Mayer-Serra published in the Mexican journal *Audiomúsica*, July 10, 1961.
16. From an interview in *Estafeta Literaria*, February 15, 1960.
17. Vinton/*Dictionary*, p.550.
18. Custer/"Contemporary," p.51.
19. Ibid., p.55.
20. Fernández-Cid/*Música*, pp.48–49.
21. Chase/*Spain*, pp.323–324.

Bibliography

Full citations for all short-title references are given in the following alphabetical listing.

Anglès/*Catálogo* Higinio Anglès and José Subirá. *Catálogo musical de la Biblioteca nacional de Madrid.* 3 vols. Barcelona: Instituto Español de Musicología, 1946–1951.

Arozamena/*Guridi* Jesús María de Arozamena. *Jesús Guridi.* Madrid: Editoria Selecta, 1967.

Arozamena/*Usandizaga* ——. *Joshemari Usandizaga y la bella epoca Donostiarra.* San Sebastián: Gráficas Izarra, 1969.

Baciero/*Albero* Antonio Baciero, ed. *Sebastián de Albero: Sonatas.* 2 vols. Madrid: Real Musical, 1978–.

Baciero/*Cuadernos* ——, ed. *Cuadernos para el piano.* Madrid: Real Musical, forthcoming.

Baciero/*Nueva Biblioteca* ——, ed. *Nueva Biblioteca de música de teclado, Siglos XVI al XVIII.* 6 vols. Madrid: Union Musical Española, 1977–.

Bergerac/*"Andalusian"* Leopold Cardona de Bergerac. "The Andalusian Music Idiom." *Music Review* 33 (1972):157–166.

Borrás/*Conrado del Campo* Tomás Borrás. *Conrado del Campo.* Madrid: Instituto Estuidos Madrileños, 1954.

Bryant/"Lesson" Celia Mae Bryant. "The Music Lesson." *Clavier* III (1964):21–26.

Carroll/"Soler" Frank Morris Carroll. "An Introduction to Soler." Ph.D. diss., University of Rochester, 1960.

CBM   *Catálogo de la Biblioteca Musical.* Madrid: Sección de cultura e información artes gráficas municipales, 1946.

Chase/"Esplá"   Gilbert Chase. "Oscar Esplá," *Monthly Musical Record* 69 (1939):199–203.

Chase/"Falla"   ———. "Falla's Music for Piano Solo." *The Chesterian* 21 (1940):41–46.

Chase/*Spain*   ———. *The Music of Spain,* 2d rev. ed. New York: W. W. Norton, 1959.

Clark/"Scarlatti"   Jane Clark. "Domenico Scarlatti and Spanish Folk Music, a Performer's Re-appraisal." *Early Music* IV (1976):19–21.

Climent/*Anglés*   José Climent, ed. *Rafael Anglés: Dos Sonatas.* Madrid: Union Musical Española, 1970.

Clough-Leighter/*Album*   Henry Clough-Leighter, ed. *Album of Ten Pieces for the Piano by Spanish Composers.* Boston: Boston Music Co., 1920.

Collet/*L'Essor*   Henri Collet. *L'Essor de la Musique Espagnole au XXe Siècle.* Paris: Max Eschig, 1929.

Crowder/"Falla"   Louis Crowder. "De Falla, A Few Portraits from the Composer's Life." *Clavier* 15 (1976):8–16, 36–37.

Custer/"Contemporary"   Arthur Custer. "Contemporary Music in Spain." In *Contemporary Music in Europe: A Comprehensive Survey,* edited by Paul Henry Lang and Nathan Broder, pp.44–60. New York: W. W. Norton, 1968.

Dean/"Turina"   Winton Dean. "Joaquin Turina." *The Chesterian* 23 (1949):92–98.

Diccionario Labor   Joaquín Pena and Higinio Anglés. *Diccionario de la música labor.* 2 vols. Barcelona: Editorial Labor, 1954.

Diego/*Música*   Gerardo Diego, et al. *Diez años de música en españa.* Madrid: Espasa Calpe, 1949.

Doderer/*Spanische*   Gerhard Doderer, ed. *Spanische und portugiesische Sonaten des 18. Jahrhunderts* (Vol. VI of *Organa Hispanica*). Heidelberg: Willy Müller, 1975.

Donostía/*Música y musicos*   José Antonio Donostía. *Música y musicos en el país vasco.* San Sebastián: Biblioteca Vascongada de los Amígos del País, 1951.

Donostía/*Música de tecla*   ———, ed. *Música de tecla en el país vasco, siglo XVIII.* San Sebastián, 1953.

Ellis/"Character Piece"   Mildred Katherine Ellis. "The French Piano Character Piece of the Nineteenth and Early Twentieth Centuries." Ph.D. diss., Indiana University, 1969.

Enciclopedia universal   *Enciclopedia universal ilustrada.* 70 vols. Madrid: Espasa-Calpe, 1958.

Eslava/"Albéniz"   Hilarión Eslava. "Biografía de Don Pedro Albéniz." *Gaceta Musical de Madrid,* April 22, 1855, pp.89–91.

Espin/"Miró" Joaquín Espin. "José Miró." *La Iberia Musical* I (1842):82–83.

Espinosa/"López" Alma Espinosa. "The Keyboard Works of Félix Máximo López (1742–1821)." Ph.D. diss., New York University, 1976.

Esteban/"Falla" Julio Esteban. "De Falla's 'Andaluza.'" *Clavier* 15 (1976):19–20.

Ferguson/*Keyboard* Howard Ferguson. *Keyboard Interpretation*. London: Oxford University Press, 1975.

Fernández-Cid/*Música* Antonio Fernández-Cid. *La música española en el siglo XX*. Madrid: Rioduero, 1973.

Fernández-Cid/*Musicos* ———. *Musicos que fueron nuestros amigos*. Madrid: Editora Nacional, 1967.

Fétis/*Biographie universelle* François-Joseph Fétis. *Biographie universelle des musiciens* . . . , 2d ed. 8 vols.; suppl., 2 vols. Paris: Firmin Didot, 1860–1865; 1878–1880.

Field/"Bagatelas" Michael Field. "Las 'Once Bagatelas' de Rodolfo Halffter." *Nuestra Música* VI (1951):44–48.

Field/"Halffter" ———. "Rodolfo Halffter and the Spanish Tradition." *The Chesterian* 27 (1953):5–8.

Field/"Segunda Sonata" ———. "La Segunda Sonata para piano, de Rodolfo Halffter." *Nuestra Música* VII (1952):208–211.

Franco/*Montsalvatge* Enrique Franco. *Montsalvatge*. Madrid: Servicio de Publicaciones del Ministerio de Educación y Ciencia, 1975.

Friedheim/"Liszt" Philip Friedheim. "The Piano Transcriptions of Liszt." *Studies in Romanticism* I (1962):83–96.

Gillespie/*Keyboard Music* John Gillespie. *Five Centuries of Keyboard Music*. Belmont, CA: Wadsworth Publishing Co., Inc., 1965.

Gillespie/"López" ———. "The Sonatas of Félix Máximo López." In *Studies in Eighteenth-Century Music,* edited by H.C. Robbins Landon. New York: Oxford University Press, 1970.

Gómez/*Latassa* Miguel Gómez Uriel. *Bibliotecas Antigua y Nueva de Escritores Aragoneses de Latassa*. 3 vols. Zaragoza: Calisto Ariño, 1884–1886.

Grove 5 Eric Blom, ed. *Grove's Dictionary of Music and Musicians,* 5th ed. 9 vols. and suppl. New York: St. Martin's Press, 1954 and 1961.

Hamilton/"Serrano" H. V. Hamilton. "Serrano." In *Grove 5*, VII:718.

Howell/*Sessé* Almonte Howell, ed. *Juan Sessé: Seis Fugas para órgano y clave*. Madrid: Union Musical Española, 1976.

Huot/"Mompou" Joanne Marie Huot. "The Piano Music of Federico Mompou (1893–)." Master's thesis, University of Washington, 1965.

Iglesias/*Mompou* Antonio Iglesias. *Federico Mompou, su obra para piano*. Madrid: Editorial Alpuerto, 1976.

Istel/"Albéniz" Edgar Istel. "Albéniz." *Musical Quarterly* 15 (1929):117–148.

Janés/*Mompou* Clara Janés. *La vida callada de Federico Mompou.* Barcelona: Editorial Ariel, 1975.

Kastner/*Silva Ibérica* Santiago Kastner, ed. *Silva Ibérica de música para tecla de los siglos XVI, XVII y XVIII.* 2 vols. Mainz: B. Schott's Söhne, 1954 and 1965.

Kirkpatrick/*Scarlatti* Ralph Kirkpatrick. *Domenico Scarlatti.* Princeton: Princeton University Press, 1953.

Larrocha/"Granados" Alicia de Larrocha. "Granados, the Composer." *Clavier* VI (1967):22–23.

Leon Tello/*Palau* Francisco José Leon Tello. *La obra pianística de Manuel Palau.* Valencia: Instituto Valenciano de Musicología, 1956.

Livermore/"Granados" Ann Livermore. "Granados and the Nineteenth Century in Spain." *Music Review* VII (1946):80–87.

Lockwood/*Notes* Albert Lockwood. *Notes on the Literature of the Piano,* 2d ed. New York: Da Capo Press, 1968.

Longyear/*Romanticism* Rey M. Longyear. *Nineteenth-Century Romanticism in Music,* 2d ed. Englewood Cliffs, N.J.: Prentice-Hall, Inc., 1973.

Lourié/"Musings" Arthur Lourié. "Musings on Music." *Musical Quarterly* 27 (1941):235–242.

Marchi/*Clavicembalisti* Giuliana Marchi, ed. *Le più belle pagine dei clavicembalisti spagnoli.* Milan: G. Ricordi, 1955.

Marco/*Música* Tomás Marco. *Música española de vanguardia.* Madrid: Ediciones Guadarrama, 1970.

Marco/"Traditionalism" ———. "Traditionalism in Contemporary Spanish Music." *World of Music* 14 (1974):30–47.

Marliave/*Etudes* Joseph de Marliave. *Etudes Musicales.* Paris; Librarie Félix Alcan, 1917.

Mast/"Albéniz" Paul Buck Mast. "Style and Structure in *Iberia* by Isaac Albéniz." Ph.D. diss., University of Rochester, 1974.

Mayer-Serra/"Nationalism" Otto Mayer-Serra. "Falla's Musical Nationalism." *Musical Quarterly* 29 (1943):1–17.

Méeus/"Mompou" Nicolás Méeus. "Federico Mompou, influences populaire et technique savante dans son oeuvre." Catholic University of Louvain (Belgium), 1967.

Mellers/"Mompou" Wilfred Mellers. "Mompou's Elegy." *The Chesterian* 26 (1952):46–54.

Mingote/*Palau* Ángel Mingote. *Manuel Palau, compositor.* Valencia: Ed. Horizontes, 1946.

Mitjana/"Espagne" Rafaël Mitjana. "La Musique en Espagne" (1914). In *Enciclopédie de la musique et dictionnaire du conservatoire.* 11 vols. Paris: Delagrave, 1913–1931.

MGG Friedrich Blume, ed. *Die Musik in Geschichte und Gegenwart.* 14 vols. and suppl. Kassel: Bärenreiter, 1949–1973.

Nadal/"Alió" Lluis B. Nadal. "Francisco Alió." *Revista Musical Catalana* V (1908).

Newman/"Goyescas" Ernest Newman. "The Granados of the Goyescas." *Musical Times* 58 (1917):343–347.

Newman/SCE William S. Newman. *The Sonata in the Classic Era.* Chapel Hill: University of North Carolina Press, 1963.

Newman/SSB ———. *The Sonata since Beethoven.* Chapel Hill: University of North Carolina Press, 1969.

Nin/Classiques Joaquín Nin, ed. *Classiques espagnols du piano. Seize Sonates* . . . and *Dix-sept Sonates et pièces anciennes d'auteurs espagnols.* 2 vols. Paris: Max Eschig, 1925 and 1929.

Pahissa/Falla Jaime Pahissa. *Vida y obra de Manuel de Falla.* Buenos Aires: Ricordi Americana, 1956.

Parada y Barreto/Diccionario José Parada y Barreto. *Diccionario técnico, histórico y biográfico de la música.* Madrid: Casa Editorial de B. Eslava, 1867.

Parris/Blasco de Nebra Robert Parris, ed. *Manuel Blasco de Nebra: Seis sonatas para clave y fuerte piano, Op. 1.* Madrid: Union Musical Española, 1964.

Parrish/"Piano" Carl G. Parrish. "The Early Piano and Its Influence on Keyboard Technique and Composition in the 18th Century." Ph.D. diss., Harvard University, 1939.

Pedrell/Antologia Felipe Pedrell, ed. *Antologia de Organistas Clasicos Españoles (Siglos XVI, XVII, y XVIII).* 2 vols. Madrid: I. Alier, 1908.

Pedrell/Catàlech ———, ed. *Catàlech de la Biblioteca musical de la Diputació de Barcelona.* 2 vols. Barcelona: Palau de la Diputació, 1908–1909.

Pedrell/Diccionario ———. *Diccionario Biográfico y Bibliográfico Músicos y Escritores de música.* Barcelona: Berdós y Feliu, 1897 (incomplete).

Pedrell/Salterio ———, ed. *Salterio Sacro Hispano.* Barcelona: Manuel Salvat.

Powell/"Cyclical" Linton E. Powell. "Cyclical Form in a Forgotten Sonata of Joaquin Turina (1882–1949)." *American Music Teacher* 26 (1977):23–25.

Powell/"Guitar Effects" ———. "Guitar Effects in Spanish Piano Music." *Piano Quarterly* 101 (Winter 1975–76):40–43.

Powell/"Halffter" ———. "Rudolfo Halffter, Domenico Scarlatti, and Kirkpatrick's Crux." *American Music Teacher* 25 (1976):4–7.

Powell/Montero ———, ed. *Joaquin Montero: Seis sonatas para clave y fuerte piano, Op. 1.* Madrid: Union Musical Española, 1977.

Powell/"Nationalists" ———. "Joaquín Turina, Another of the Spanish Nationalists." *Clavier* 15 (1976):28–30.

Powell/"Rhythms" ———. "The Influence of Dance Rhythms on the

Piano Music of Joaquin Turina." *Music Review* 37 (1976):143–151.

Powell/"Spain" ———. "The Piano Music of Spain (Joaquin Turina)." *Piano Quarterly* 102 (Summer 1977):45–48.

Powell/"Turina" ———. "The Piano Music of Joaquin Turina (1882–1949)." Ph.D. diss., University of North Carolina, 1974.

Pujol/*Mestres* David Pujol, ed. *Mestres de l'escolania de Montserrat, Música instrumental.* 2 vols. Monestir de Montserrat, 1934 and 1936.

Ruiz-Pipó/*Montero* Antonio Ruiz-Pipó, ed. *Joaquin Montero: Diez minuetes para clave y fuerte piano.* Madrid: Union Musical Española, 1973.

Ruiz-Pipó/*Música vasca* ———, ed. *Música vasca del siglo XVIII para tecla.* Madrid: Union Musical Española, 1972.

Salazar/*Música* Adolfo Salazar. *La música contemporánea en españa.* Madrid: Ediciones la Nave, 1930.

Salazar/*El Siglo* Adolfo Salazar. *El Siglo Romántico.* Madrid: J.M. Yagües, 1936.

Saldoni/*Diccionario* Baltasar Saldoni. *Diccionario biográfico-bibliográfico de efemérides de musicos españoles.* 4 vols. Madrid: Imprenta de Antonio Pérez Dubrull, 1868–1881.

Scholes/*Burney* Percy Scholes, ed. *Dr. Burney's Musical Tours in Europe* II. London: Oxford University Press, 1959.

Sheveloff/"Scarlatti" Joel Leonard Sheveloff. "The Keyboard Music of Domenico Scarlatti: A Re-evaluation of the Present State of Knowledge in the Light of the Sources." Ph.D. diss., Brandeis University, 1970.

Sopeña/*Historia* Federico Sopeña. *Historia de la música española contemporánea.* Madrid: Ediciones Rialp, 1958.

Sopeña/*Rodrigo* ———. *Joaquin Rodrigo.* Madrid: Ediciones y Publicaciones Españolas, 1946.

Sopeña/*Turina* ———. *Joaquin Turina* 2d. ed. Madrid: Editora Nacional, 1956.

Starkie/"Mompou" Walter Starkie. "Mompou." In *Grove 5*, V:825–826.

Starkie/*Spain* ———. *Spain.* 2 vols. Geneva: Edisli, 1958.

Subirá/*Historia* José Subirá. *Historia de la música española e hispanoamericana.* Barcelona: Salvat Editores, 1953.

Trend/"Alió" John B. Trend. "Alió." In *Grove 5*, I:110.

Trend/"Falla" ———. "Falla." In *Grove 5*, III:11–12.

Trend/*Spanish* ———. *Manuel de Falla and Spanish Music.* New York: Alfred A. Knopf, 1929.

Valls/*Música* Manuel Valls. *La música catalana contemporánea.* Barcelona: Editorial Selecta, 1960.

Van Vechten/*Excavations* Carl Van Vechten. *Excavations.* New York: Alfred A. Knopf, 1926.

Villar/*Músicos I*   Rogelio Villar. *Músicos españoles*. Vol. I. Madrid: Ediciones Mateu, 1918.

Vinton/*Dictionary*   John Vinton, ed. *Dictionary of Contemporary Music*. New York: E. P. Dutton and Co., 1971.

Vuillermoz/*Musiques*   Émile Vuillermoz. *Musiques d'aujourd'hui: Artistes d'hier et d'aujourd'hui*. Paris: Les Éditions G. Cres et Cie., 1923.

Wirth/"Falla"   Helmut Wirth. "Falla." In *MGG* III:1747–1758.

Index